The Best 100 Free Apps for Libraries

Jim Hahn

The Scarecrow Press, Inc.
Lanham • Toronto • Plymouth, UK
2013

Published by Scarecrow Press, Inc.
A wholly owned subsidiary of The Rowman & Littlefield Publishing Group, Inc.
4501 Forbes Boulevard, Suite 200, Lanham, Maryland 20706
www.rowman.com

10 Thornbury Road, Plymouth PL6 7PP, United Kingdom

British Cataloging in Publication Information Available

Library of Congress Cataloging-in-Publication Data
The best 100 free apps for libraries / Jim Hahn.
    p. cm
  Includes index.
  ISBN 978-0-8108-8582-0 (pbk.) — ISBN 978-0-8108-8583-7 (electronic) 1. Mobile communication systems—Library applications. 2. Public services (Libraries)—Technological innovations. 3. Application software—Directories. I. Hahn, Jim, 1979– II. Title: Best one hundred free apps for libraries.
  Z680.5.B47 2013
  005.3—dc23   2013003620

∞™ The paper used in this publication meets the minimum requirements of American National Standard for Information Sciences—Permanence of Paper for Printed Library Materials, ANSI/NISO Z39.48-1992.

Printed in the United States of America

For my Dad, who taught me to work,
and Mom, who taught me why.

Contents

Preface

The Best 100 Free Apps for Libraries is for those librarians who want to know more about apps but do not necessarily own a smartphone or develop apps. This book is also for librarians who do not envision purchasing a smartphone. Essentially, it is for the beginner, the librarian who is content with his or her basic cell phone. This is a perfectly acceptable position for general librarians. You should know that devices like the iPhone couldn't wholly replicate all library services.

The apps covered here are tools that could free up librarian time and in effect allow librarians to focus on other areas needing their expertise. Treat this book as a sort of annotated bibliography for apps. I'll identify sources that you may want to recommend to patrons. You'll be up-to-date on app functionality if you give this book even a cursory look. This book will then also save you the time of sifting through the numerous apps available on the application stores.

Apps aren't really complicated at all. An app is simply a lightweight software component added on to the mobile device after purchase. The application store is the place where you can select and load a mobile app onto your device. This book focuses on those apps that are freely available on these application stores.

Innovative library services and information access occur in a number of ways with apps, depending on the devices, software, and infrastructures used. One useful framework is to think of the device as the various hardware components it consists of: the camera on the phone along with different wireless capabilities, like WiFi access. This will give you a sense of what is possible and feasible to accomplish with mobile software. I detail a little more about this approach and also the mobile ecosystem in chapter

1, which covers how to stay current in the mobile app world and suggests resources for finding out about apps that may come along after this book is published, as well as professional groups within the American Library Association that you can participate in at conferences and online.

Chapter 2 begins the review of apps by typology with a review of utility apps, those apps that provide quick access and views of information, like the popular suite of language translation apps often requested by students. Continuing the reviews of apps by type is chapter 3, which details immersive apps, or augmented reality applications. The immersive components have parallels with gaming applications and basically create graphical information overlays through the camera feed onto the view of the surrounding environment.

For those looking to boost their knowledge on practical or productive apps, see chapter 4, which covers the productivity realm of mobile software. Chapter 5 is the final app review chapter and it reports on the world of mobile social applications like Facebook and Twitter, and their integration with mobile and library services.

You may be pleased to know that it isn't necessary to read this book linearly from front to back. This book can actually be read by starting in any app type. You could start at the last chapter, in social applications, if that is your interest. Alternatively, you could just jump into the middle of the book with immersive augmented reality apps and start reading about an app type and computing possibility you never knew existed. While the apps in each section are organized by type, there is no one way to read this book.

Treat this work as a sort of reference guide to the mobile apps available for library services. It may give you ideas for apps to suggest to your patrons, to use in your work, or to provide enhanced outreach and engagement to your user population. If you are thinking of purchasing a tablet device for your library, many of the use cases in the book detail ideas for making use of tablets in service offerings of the library.

Chapter 1

Staying Current in the Mobile App World

Narrowly focused technology books run the risk of obsolescence; this introduction will discuss strategies for mitigating this concern.

It seems that technologies come and go every day—certainly, new mobile applications are arriving all the time. The rapid maturation of mobile software is underscored by the hundreds of thousands of applications available and also by the billions of mobile applications downloaded by smartphone owners.

As an indication of the popularity of apps, note that the Apple iTunes App Store has over 500,000 apps available, with over 25 billion downloads as of March 2012. The Android app store, Google Play (https://play.google.com/about/features/), indicates it has 450,000 apps available to users, with over 10 billion downloads (source: http://www.informationweek.com/news/mobility/smart_phones/232601991).

It seems just when we've grown accustomed to the current high-tech landscape, something new comes along and we must adapt. As librarians, this happens to be the information environment we have come to expect in the digital era. And yet, the new information environments have achieved a kind of hyper-state of change and revision. Is it too much to keep up now?

It isn't too much if you know what to look for—great free apps have a couple of fairly basic combinations. The hardware of the phone— the GPS, the WiFi, the camera—and the way these components combine with other sources of data are what creates novel software approaches. Let's take a look at a really popular app that was recently in the news: Instagram.

The Instagram app (http://instagr.am/) enables the user to create fun, interesting overlays of vintage coloring (filters) for their phone photos. The integration of the Instagram app with other online services, like commenting sites, makes it easier to share information from the app as well. So in the example of Instagram, we see data sharing enabled by the data capture of the camera—it is the creative and innovative mix of these software and hardware elements that makes this a compelling and popular app. It is one of the most popular free apps available.

The strategy employed will be to detail how each app is making use of the phone's software, hardware, and infrastructure capabilities. This book includes in each review a use case for the app, and alternative use cases where appropriate. This is followed with a statement on how apps of this type will evolve in the future. Each review will offer a treatment of historical continuity with previous apps.

Common themes that continue to surface in the review of the 100 best free apps follow a few trends. These trends range from the basic emulation of popular websites to the key Google tools of voice search, gesture search, and search by media, as well as trends in the social and interactive apps. It isn't solely social apps that are seeing innovation for pooling users' social networks. Many apps reviewed in this book do feature social integration—posting to your Facebook timeline, push notification (alerts that pop up from your app), and a variety of media that includes images, but also video and streaming audio.

Many of the use cases presented here also discuss tablet computing, leisurely reading in a library setting, and the tablet as a tool in the librarian's toolkit, both for staying current on news in technology and science and other topics, but also as a means of staying connected while in embedded or offsite roles. A number of the social networking tools can help to connect users at a distance with activities and facilities of the library. One of the most basic and sensible tools for the integration of apps is the ability for image content to be uploaded directly from the mobile application.

The question that we return to, from the preface: how do libraries stay current when the app world remains a shifting target? Certainly panning through the most popular apps over a given period will help. In addition to this, regularly observing what tools your patrons are making use of will help guide your information services. It also makes sense to rethink how your work at a distance, in the library, or within installations of the library building could be helped by emerging software tools. One of the strengths of mobile computing is that the software can become more feature-rich as time goes on. In the course of writing this book, nearly half of the apps that I reviewed actually featured updates and bug fixes. This happened in less than a five-month time span—this is encouraging and, at the same time, a bit dizzying.

Something like mobile technology applications in library settings actually changes what library services and information access may mean. In a sense this book is taking a refocusing approach to mobile services. Mobile services alter our traditional definitions of collections. They change what it means to provide access to a certain type of collection. Different library services change how we lay out a library facility—which might now include the option of tablet kiosks. Finally, mobile serices may change how we work, as much as they have changed how we live. For now, the future of library services with mobile devices is bright, so long as the integration of information access moves forward as a component of the information environments that our patron base is using, this is a place in which the librarians and information professionals must also participate.

In order to track ongoing developments, try searching for the most popular apps from app stores. These websites can be periodically analyzed for emerging trends in this field. The "Genius" feature in iTunes can recommend similar apps based on apps an individual has found useful. The Google Play store (https://play.google.com/store) has an "apps like this" facet. Use these sources to follow the very latest mobile app developments. Additional resources you will want to periodically consult include:

- M-libraries Wiki: http://www.libsuccess.org/index.php?title=M-Libraries
- Gadget Lab: http://www.wired.com/gadgetlab/
- NYT's Gadgetwise Blog: http://gadgetwise.blogs.nytimes.com
- ALA Connect, Mobile Computing Interest Group (LITA): http://connect.ala.org/node/72768

Chapter 2

Utility Apps for Library Services

Utility apps are those that provide quick views of information.

Popular apps in this category are similar in interface display and performance to the native weather, compass, or calculator apps on an iPhone. As a comparison to Android and iPhone functionalities, the map applications that come loaded standard on both systems are examples of utility applications.

We begin our first review of the chapter with translator tools, which are popular, in-demand apps by students, particularly those in their first year of undergraduate study. A few apps for development that may be useful in a library setting is an "available computers" app, "available study" room notification, and even availability of technology resources in the library.

Chapter 2

ADOBE READER

Screenshot:

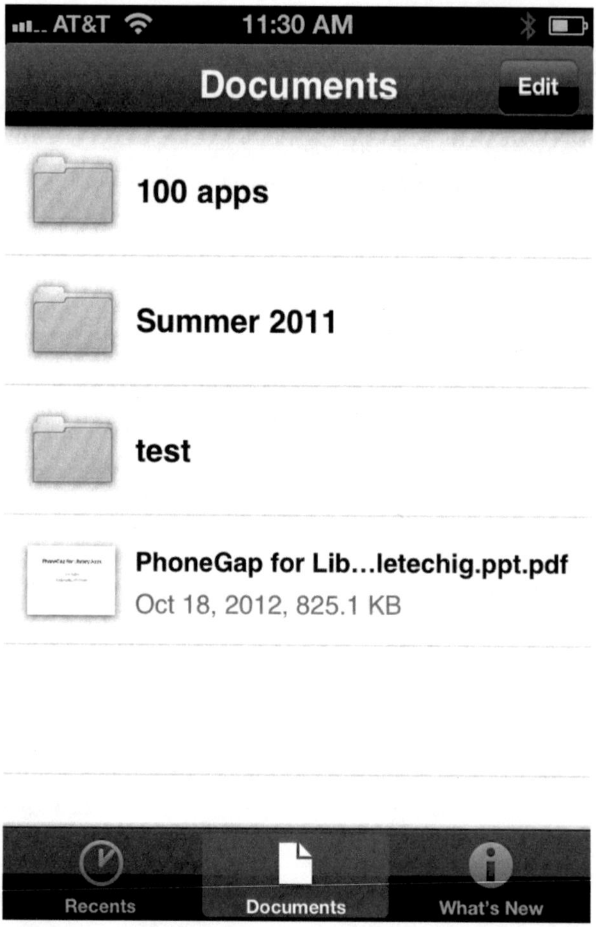

Figure 2.1.   Adobe Reader. The app includes helpful folder organization for document management on your mobile device.

What it does: This is the free PDF viewing app by industry leader Adobe.
There are already existing integration features for some PDF viewing in
mobile platforms. For example, with the app loaded, when a user accesses
a PDF within another website in the iOS operating system the "view in
. . ." option will prompt the user to view the PDF inside Adobe Reader.
With the Adobe Reader app, the option to use standard industry tools for
viewing PDFs will create a familiar document-viewing experience.

The Adobe Reader supports text search within the document; you can highlight as well as create annotations. Additionally, you can use the form-complete tool to complete and email forms. The reader tool is a fully featured Adobe product that allows you to do pretty much all of the Adobe functions you are accustomed to completing in the standard desktop Adobe product. The home screen of the Adobe app is organized for document viewing, with a simple "recents" tab, as well as a "documents" tab of all your Adobe documentation. Finally, the app comes loaded with a helpful "Getting Started" sample PDF with information on app functionality.

Use case: Your library patrons will no doubt be making use of email through their mobile devices. When library users get attachments, they may need to easily and quickly read or edit the PDF attachments. In order to edit these PDFs they usually need to complete a form. The Adobe Reader app supports form completion.

Additional use case: The documents tab of the Adobe Reader app also supports file-organization tasks. You or your library patrons may be getting a large number of files and PDFs coming into your mobile device—downloading these to your iOS device may pose a problem, since at present the iOS system doesn't have a desktop/file system that is comparable to the desktop services. This is a gap that the Adobe Reader app can help bridge, since with the Adobe app you are able to create and manage folders of PDFs. While this isn't the only mobile app on the market that can do so, it is one of the more feature-rich PDF viewers available from the app store.

What you should know/more information about how it works: Functionality that is similar to that of the Adobe desktop version is available here; so if you are familiar with the standard annotation tools, the mobile application will be easy to use. A particularly useful feature in the Adobe app viewer is the ability to see where you are in the total document with a slider function in the screen—you can use this slider function to select your desired page in the document. A helpful bookmark feature is also present in the app—it allows you to save a page to come back to, which is certainly helpful for navigating in the mobile interface.

Apps like this to look out for in the future: This is certainly in line with some of the more feature-rich apps that mimic productivity-level applications. The mobile device capabilities that allow users to be productive, like the Adobe application, will likely become more commonplace.

Consulted: https://itunes.apple.com/app/adobe-reader/id469337564?mt=8

AUTISM APP

Screenshot:

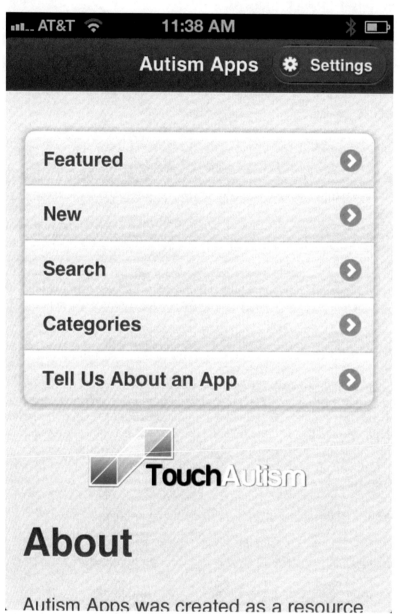

Figure 2.2.   Autism App. The main home screen and function of this app is to aggregate the apps that will be of use to special populations.

What it does: This app is an aggregate of other apps. It collects, organizes, and helps users find other special population mobile resources. The app is organized as follows on the front screen, by way of a list-view menu: "featured," "new," "search," "categories," and "tell us about an app." A very useful component/filter is the settings button in the upper right corner—where you can filter apps suggested by app type (free or paid) and app device (iPad or iPod). Finally there is a sort function which enables you to view them by name, price, or the "star rating" on the app store.

Use case: Librarians in need of a resource to consult for spectrum disorder–type apps will want to consult the Autism app for free content that can be useful to this population. While doing an iTunes search could be useful, actually loading this app onto an iPad or iPhone for patron use will help them to discover apps on their own that serve this population.

Additional use case: How these tools are actually useful for the populations they are designed for will rest on actually downloading and making the apps available to the populations. If your library has special resources, or is a special library for delivering resources to populations such as these, then it makes sense to make available this content from a mobile device such as a library-owned iPad or tablet and actually gather use feedback to begin to form an understanding of the viability of these apps.

What you should know/more information about how it works: As an app that provides information about other apps, the Autism app acts a little like traditional reference sources in that regard, providing source material that points to other apps of interest.

Apps like this to look out for in the future: It is rare on the iTunes Store to see an app that acts as an app aggregator. There isn't a lot of precedent for using an app to identify other apps, since that is what the iTunes App Store does. However, with educational aspects and special populations outreach and services, there may be a bit of a shift in how these apps get made and delivered to users. What this means is that we'll want to be on the lookout in the future for educational apps that seem to function more like aggregators of content than providers of content.

Consulted: https://itunes.apple.com/us/app/autism-apps/id441600681?mt=8

BARCODE SCANNER (ANDROID)

Screenshot:

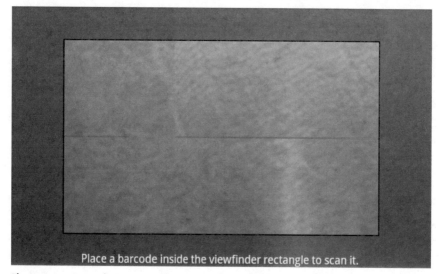

Place a barcode inside the viewfinder rectangle to scan it.

Figure 2.3. Barcode Scanner. The app works by placing a library barcode inside of the scan region (the rectangular area) to scan.

What it does: This is a basic barcode scanner that allows you to scan item barcodes to search for those items on the web. You can send the barcode information to a Google Book Search. If the barcode is recognized you can select among the following tabs: product search, book search, or book content search, or send the barcode information to the Google Shopper app—a helpful price comparison tool.

The Barcode Scanner app for Android is also a plugin for other apps that are making use of the open source code from this project to incorporate the Barcode Scanner into their apps.

Use case: Library users will be interested in checking out this Barcode Scanner app for their trips to bookstores or while browsing your library book stacks. They will be able to read item summaries where available for the books in Google Book Search. With the product search functionality, library users can compare the prices for books in nearby stores. The "use my location" function will be activated here in the Google product search to indicate where the book (or other product) may be purchased nearby.

Additional use case: For those librarians who work in academic environments the barcode scanner could be used for orientation and scavenger hunt–type activities. With a little imagination of services staff, the games can ask students to search through book stacks to bring back the highest-value book in the collection—or the book that contains the highest starred review in Google Books Search. These activities will help your new users become familiar with the stacks, including book locations and popular areas, as well as let the students tell each other which areas of the library book stacks are interesting and relevant to their studies.

What you should know/more information about how it works: The Barcode Scanner works through your smartphone's camera—you have to be in good lighting for this to work, and the app also requires that you have a decent camera. Some Android tablets come with camera components that do not have autofocus capability; a tablet without autofocus would not be able to make use of this app.

Apps like this to look out for in the future: Future apps that use camera input and redisplay information will likely be along the lines of augmented reality applications. Augmented reality applications are interactive and allow graphics to be inserted into the camera view onto objects in the surrounding environment in real time.

Consulted: https://play.google.com/store/apps/details?id=com.google .zxing.client.android

Chapter 2

CARDSTAR

Screenshot:

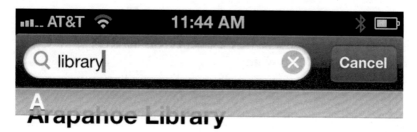

Figure 2.4.   CardStar. The app is populated with participating institutions and the user can locate an institution from the search screen.

What it does: Here is where you can store all your card information, like your library card, or bookstore/bookseller cards. The app bills itself as "your mobile loyalty card manager"; you simply add a card by scanning it with your phone's camera. Then the app is used during checkout when you would normally scan a plastic version of your card—you can now just scan the digital copy of the plastic. A number of libraries (mostly public) have added their names to the "merchants" list in the card-storing portion of the app. Once you load in various reward cards you can also browse through any special offers that pertain to these cards.

Use case: The obvious library use of CardStar is to allow your patrons to check out library material from this app. Rather than having your patrons bring a plastic card to the library with them, consider allowing checkouts with this mobile app featuring a digital copy of their card.

Additional use case: An additional use case for libraries that are interested in experimenting with the "rewards paradigm" would be to make a new summer book club reward for young adults or teen programs. This may be a way to introduce populations that don't normally get engaged in library programs to have a gamified approach to engaging with library events. It would work like this: you provide digital cards that your student or young adult participants have on their CardStar app—when they obtain a certain level of pages read, they can redeem awards using the library award card stored in their phone.

What you should know/more information about how it works: You should know that in order for this app to be useful you actually have to add your card information; you cannot just look up your plastic rewards card and find your subscription in the database. So there is an initial outlay of setting up the CardStar with your personal card information—but the more information you add the more useful the CardStar will be. Just put all your plastic rewards cards in and free your keychain of them forever.

Apps like this to look out for in the future: The mobile payments arena is young but growing, so in the future not only will you be able to process your rewards and check out from your phone, but paying for items from your mobile device will become increasingly popular. It stands to reason, in fact, that more and more payments will be processed by mobile devices in the coming years. So this is an area to watch for e-commerce especially.

Consulted: https://itunes.apple.com/us/app/cardstar/id301460311?mt=8

CONVERT FREE

Screenshot:

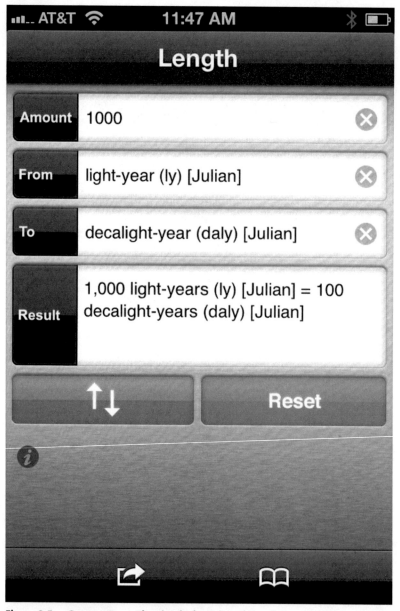

Figure 2.5.   Convert Free. The simple form interface allows you to set amounts and see results quickly in one view.

What it does: This is a free conversion tool for the iOS platform. It features an easy-to-understand autocomplete tool in which you type in the units you want to convert. There is also a "show list" feature where the user can pan through all of the available units supported. You can also email or bookmark the conversions after you have made the calculations so that you can refer to commonly needed or important conversions at a later time. According to the iTunes App Store there are over 5,000 units in the converter.

Use case: This could be a useful patron tool in special or science-specific library locations. The Convert Free app could be used to replace commonly used reference sources in the sciences like conversion tables, or currency conversion websites. Patrons visiting other countries may be able to make multiple uses of the unit conversions if they need to convert distances from one set of units to another, and they can also convert their home or familiar currency to that of the country they are currently visiting.

What you should know/more information about how it works: The app also is able to download specific currency conversion rates for getting fairly up-to-date currency transfer rates. Converting from dollars to other units is fairly easy with the autocomplete functionality of the application—meaning you don't have to type out the full currency, rather you can view the autosuggestions and choose from a suggested list of currencies based on the first letter of the currency that the user entered.

Apps like this to look out for in the future: As utility apps, conversion tools are useful when they are programmed to learn from previous searches and surface the most commonly converted types of searches. Look for more intelligent searching from these tools in the future using machine learning algorithms and other smart searching tools.

Consulted: https://itunes.apple.com/us/app/convert-any-unit/id46518 0749?ls=1&mt=8

THE CONGRESSIONAL RECORD

Screenshot:

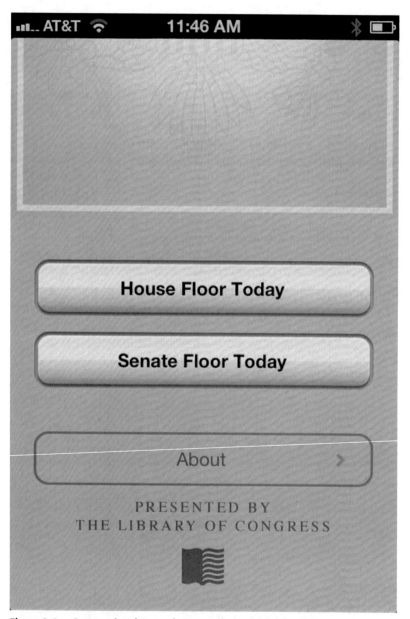

Figure 2.6.   Congressional Record. Access the activities for the House or Senate floor for the current day by way of the Library of Congress.

What it does: With a search scope beginning in 1995 (the 104th Congress), the Congressional Record iPhone app provides access to all subsequent congressional records. The app allows searching inside of congressional reports. Features of the Congressional Record app include access to a daily digest, a Senate section, a House section, an extension of remarks section, and the option to view an entire issue of the Congressional Record. Further, you can view the contents of "House Floor Today" and "Senate Floor Today" from the app home screen.

Use case: For younger library patrons, searching government information resources may not be an area of sustained interest. However, with a mobile interface to the Congressional Record, there may be inroads that librarians can make for delivering government information to this group. Mobile platforms are compelling and interesting for the millennial cohort. Librarians can suggest this resource in workshops on government information or even at the reference desk.

What you should know/more information about how it works: There is a comprehensive "about" section in the application that helps users understand more about the organization of content and provides a helpful definition for each tab. Users who are new to congressional data will have a guide to understanding the structure of each document. One of the downsides to using this app is that the information presents in a full-page document view, and hasn't been rendered for small-screen viewing. As a result, iPhone viewing may prove slightly cumbersome, but on larger-screen devices like the iPad or even iPad mini, this will not be as problematic.

Apps like this to look out for in the future: Open governmental information may continue to expand as agencies look for more efficient ways to reach out to the public with their data. Increasing the accessibility of day-to-day government information is a noteworthy and important service offering to watch, particularly as it begins to incorporate new delivery modes like mobile device platforms.

Consulted: https://itunes.apple.com/us/app/the-congressional-record/id492077075?mt=8

DRAGON DICTATION

Screenshot:

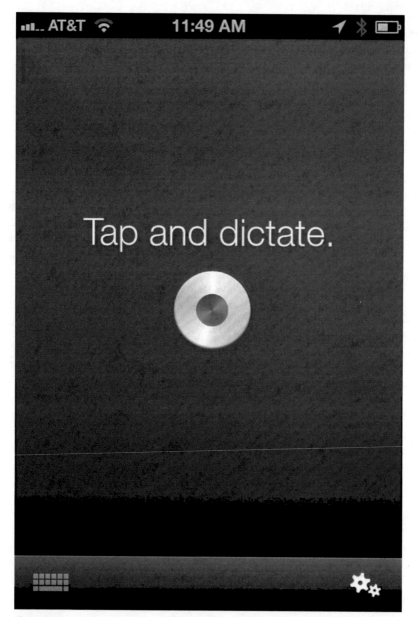

Figure 2.7.   Dragon Dictation. This simple, easy-to-use interface is a one-touch dictation tool.

What it does: This app features voice recognition software. This app is useful for when you need to record ideas or send messages, but are either unwilling or do not have the time to type on a keyboard. From the voice-recognized text, you can send an email or a text message. The iTunes App Store listing for the dictation software claims that dictation is five times faster than typing on the iPhone. The Dragon Dictation app has functionality to post your dictated message to your social networking accounts such as your Facebook timeline or Twitter feeds. As a bonus the app offers a selection of languages, so if your native language is not English, you can still make use of the dictation functionality.

Use case: This app could be a useful way to send yourself reminders while on or away from the research desk—librarians are often juggling multiple priorities and are not always able to send the email they need to send; with a Dragon Dictation mobile app loaded onto their phones, they could quickly send reminders to themselves about messages they need to follow up on. You may want to consider making use of Dragon Dictation to send short emails that don't require tons of research or additional thinking.

Additional use case: For your users—you may want to suggest Dragon Dictation as a way to receive collection requests from your users.

What you should know/more information about how it works: On first load, the app asks if it can use your current location. This is not for use within social networks or anything that it posts in your email about location. The location sharing is activated because the app is trying to learn and recognize regional dialects or inflections over time—enabling location sharing may improve the recognition for you and others in your area. The app works on voice recognition—and fairly accurate recognition of your voice as well. If you find that there are errors in the words that have been transcribed, you can edit the message with the standard keyboard on the iPhone.

Apps like this to look out for in the future: Future implementation of voice recognition software may be more commonplace—this app developer seems to have found a way to make accurate text-based uses of voice recognition. New uses will be to actually interact with other apps—not just Siri (iPhone's native voice recognition tool), but apps that provide functionalities.

Consulted: https://itunes.apple.com/us/app/dragon-dictation/id341446 764?mt=8

DROPBOX

Screenshot:

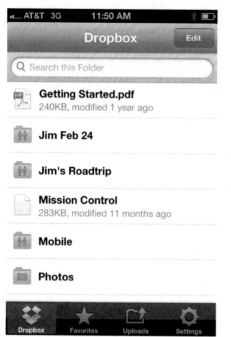

Figure 2.8. Dropbox. The app interface allows a user to see all the content of their Dropbox account.

What it does: This app is the iPhone gateway into the popular Internet-based sharing site http://www.dropbox.com; most librarians have heard of Dropbox or may already have a Dropbox account. If you've never heard of it before, you could surf over and consult its help pages to learn more, but the rundown is fairly basic functionality: the web version allows you to quickly drag and drop files into your web-based folder on any computer. Additionally, you would then have quick access to the contents of the Dropbox folder from any computer. Enter the iPhone, a computer with less storage than the common desktop system. Even the iPad with its productivity-based overhaul still lacks the desktop-like file system and folder hierarchy that we've become accustomed to on our desktop computers. With the iPhone app, you'll have access to all the folders that you've previously dropped files into. How is this useful on the go? That is a good question. We cover that next.

Use case: Suppose you are viewing a PDF from your mobile device—not the greatest experience, really—but you wanted to get it to your project team back at the office since there seems to be some actionable data here that they need to move on. In order to get things moving you can drop the PDF into a shared folder that the rest of your team will be able to quickly access, once they are notified you have shared the folder with them.

Consider also that you might be on the train and want to consult that very important spreadsheet. You knew, you just knew you were going to need to consult it later, so you dropped it into your Dropbox, thinking that definitely, when you got to the hotel later, you would be able to log in and retrieve it—but now you have a need for immediacy; what if the hotel doesn't have a computer? You could log in to the Dropbox app and access the folders that are already existing files in your account.

Additional use cases: The iPhone's camera-to-Dropbox integration is the latest release. This allows you to upload camera photos directly to a Dropbox folder. This may be useful for those who want to share photo files with a group or with a team outside of the traditional online social networking platform tools that the iPhone integrates with. Consider making use of the favorites module of the Dropbox app.

*Favorites: You can star any Dropbox favorites in the app for offline viewing. Do this for those files you know you will need to access later, or for mission-critical documents, ones that you'll still want access to if your data plan stops functioning suddenly.

What you should know/more information about how it works: As I intimated in the favorites section, you will of course mostly need to have access to a data plan/WiFi connection of some kind in order to ensure full functionality of the app, but this service considers that some files may be more important to you than others, and for those situations, the favorites modules will be important. Also, the app becomes fairly intuitive to use once you have logged into the standard desktop version, so make sure you understand the desktop service before thinking the app pointless.

Apps like this to look out for in the future: Cloud-based services are getting to be pretty commonplace. For those users of Google Docs, you'll want to be aware of a service coming online known as Google Drive. The Google Drive is desktop and mobile integration of the popular Google Docs feature. Google doesn't currently offer the Google Docs feature for the iPhone, so the Dropbox app is not going to see competition right now in this domain. Android users, on the other hand, will have access to Google Drive from the Google Play store.

Consulted: http://www.dropbox.com

FING

Screenshot:

Figure 2.9.   Fing. The app will show you the names and IP addresses of wireless networks that your mobile device can access.

What it does: This app can locate and identify all devices that are currently connected to a WiFi access point. You can email yourself the identified access points nearest you as well. You can basically discover what networks are around you and then analyze those networks with this application.

Use case: A library that contains WiFi access points will likely get questions regarding connectivity. With an app such as Fing you are able to ping and find your access points in the library. Pinging access points in your library is useful to getting a sense of overall connectivity, and then you can also learn more about the traffic that is currently on your network by using the Fing app.

Additional use case: There may be applications for using this app in home environments as well. Since your library patrons may be interested, or have questions about troubleshooting their home network, this app could help identify all the devices that are connected to a home network and then also monitor them.

What you should know/more information about how it works: According to the documentation from the Overlook Soft website (http://overlooksoft .com/fing) the app works best on Ethernet and WiFi networks.

Apps like this to look out for in the future: Many more devices in the future will also include Internet connectivity. Apps like the Fing app could be quite useful for troubleshooting the connectivity and also possible network performance or non-functioning appliances in the Internet of the future.

Consulted: https://itunes.apple.com/us/app/fing-network-scanner/ id430921107?mt=8

GOOGLE CHROME

Screenshot:

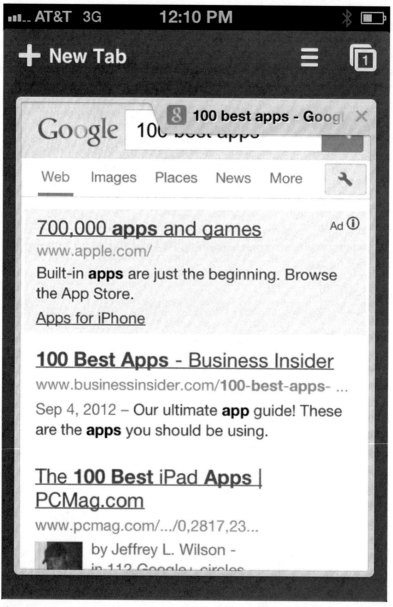

Figure 2.10. Google Chrome. Tabbed browsing is available through the Google Chrome app.

What it does: The popular web browser by Google comes to the mobile interface. Along with this port to the mobile environment comes some of the standard functionality Chrome users expect. Features include dynamic autocomplete functionality. Another option in the Google Chrome browser includes the ability to sign in to the mobile browser; by signing in to Chrome you can transfer any of your bookmarks from your desktop browser to your mobile device.

Use case: For librarians who work in multiple office locations or service points making use of the Google Chrome app can help to make accessible your bookmarks and tabs across browsing platforms. If, for example, you are using a tablet at one reference point or embedded location, you may want to consider signing in to your Google Chrome account in order to provide ubiquitous access to your work tools and settings. Bookmarks you may want access to include any reference pages, departmental resources, virtual chat services, and other library service–specific web interfaces.

Additional use case: Your patron base may also be completing work or professional tasks on their mobile devices. These tasks may be made easier and more efficiently completed should your library users have access to their settings on their desktop system.

What you should know/more information about how it works: With the Google Chrome app you are able to make use of the voice search functionality— this may be useful when searching on the go and when typing on the keyboard interface is not possible.

Apps like this to look out for in the future: Features like data portability and integration among multiple devices, from your desktop system to your mobile system, are going to see more innovation in the future. One can expect to see more apps that will do such integrative sharing as the Chrome open tabs. Future iterations of browser apps should be designed without requiring a login. Login times on a mobile device can be time consuming and may not work at the moment when they are needed.

Consulted: https://itunes.apple.com/us/app/chrome/id535886823?mt=8

GOOGLE GESTURE SEARCH (ANDROID)

Screenshot:

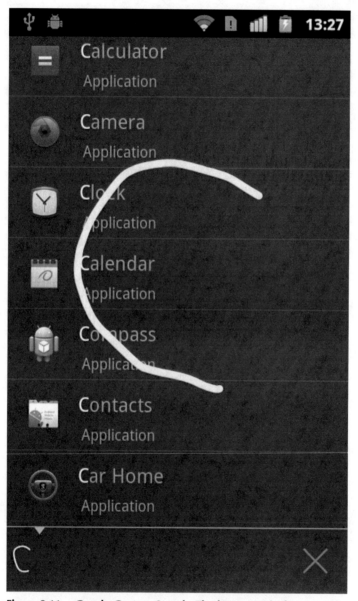

Figure 2.11.   Google Gesture Search. The letter "C" is drawn on the interface of the mobile phone, and the app then performs a device-wide search for items that begin with this letter.

What it does: This app is set up so that you can draw the first letter of a search query onto your phone's screen. The app will interpret your character and display results that the program interprets as relevant to your search query. The search operates by turning your gesture into a letter and then attempting to match this letter across content that is stored in your phone. The app is essentially an Android phone search tool—searching across your contact list and downloaded applications, it can also search music and bookmarks on the Android mobile device.

Use case: Consider the user that has downloaded nearly 100 of the free apps from this book—searching through the list of apps on their device can become time intensive or unsafe even, if the user is looking for an app while they are otherwise occupied. Just set this app on the home screen of your phone and access it quickly and efficiently—finally just scribble with your finger the first letter in the app you are looking to load and the app will deliver search results over your letter-based scribble query.

Additional use case: Alternatively, librarians who have extra time and development resources may be interested in incorporating the gesture search code into their mobile app. The Google Gesture Search code is available to incorporate into Android applications from here: http://code.google.com/p/gesture-search-api-demo/.

What you should know/more information about how it works: For an app like this to work and be useful to you, your drawings onto the phone interface need to resemble as closely as possible the character in the term that you are looking for. Additionally, the app requests permission to send your gestures to Google for mining and improving their recognition algorithms. If you don't want your scribbles and the search results you selected sent along to Google then do not select this feature. The app should theoretically be improving over time as it learns that the resulting information is useful based on your gestures and subsequent selections.

Apps like this to look out for in the future: If proponents of the "Internet of things" are correct then in the future of computing everyday consumer electronics will be connected to the net by IP addresses. The future of everyday consumer electronics being networked will lead to new input mechanisms for queries that will move users away from keyboard-based input—which is actually just a crude re-use of a typewriter-based paradigm. The gesture-based computing of the future will most likely manifest in areas outside of mobile apps.

Consulted: http://www.google.com/mobile/gesture-search/; https://play.google.com/store/apps/details?id=com.google.android.apps.gesturesearch

GOOGLE TRANSLATE FOR MOBILE

Screenshot:

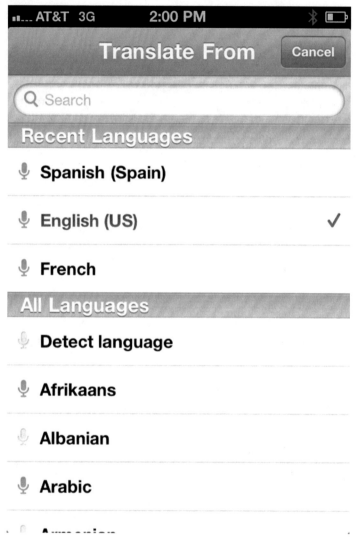

Figure 2.12.   Google Translate. The user can choose a language or the app can also auto-detect the source language to translate.

What it does: This app is the mobile version of Google's online translator tool. You can type or speak a word into the app and get a translation in your language of choice.

Use case: With the Google Translate app users are able to supplement, if not simply replace, the language dictionaries we have in the reference collections of the library. Generally, library users are already making heavy use of online translating tools, which they can use to copy and paste in foreign words and understand their meaning.

The mobile value-add for this service is the voice-to-app search—you can speak into the phone and the voice recognition software will translate your speech to another language. Not all languages are supported by a voice translate lookup, though we can probably expect Google to improve upon the number of languages that are supported in the speak-to-translate domain. This app is as fairly bare bones as they come, but the compelling quick lookup on the go is extremely useful.

The use case here is pretty much that users can speak or type in the terms or phrases that they want translated—much like the webpage lookup. A helpful "starred" icon lets you star words and translations that you can quickly reference again.

Additional use case: For those library patrons who are getting ready to take a vacation or visit a new country, this application can be as useful as picking up travel guides from the library. Suggesting this to patrons before they leave for trips would help them identify common everyday words they will need to know.

What you should know/more information about how it works: If you are already familiar with the web version of Google Translate picking up this resource will be easy. For those who haven't used it, the translate page (http://translate.google.com/) will not take too long to become familiar.

Apps like this to look out for in the future: In the future, apps like this will have language support for a broad range of options. It is theorized that users can expect that instead of speaking the words to the phone, the phone will be able to do voice-to-speech and also make use of the camera portion of the phone for text input. The optical character recognition research that Google is hosting (http://code.google.com/p/tesseract-ocr/) makes it seem as though the input for the phone can someday come from your camera—most likely it will be Google, or a startup that Google purchases, that could make this type of search by media a reality.

In the future, developers may begin to incorporate the Google Translate app into other apps, so while you see the app as a standalone service in this current iteration, future interaction with the Google Translate service may come from within an application that is pulling functionality, essentially using the service as a plugin to power some other portion of an app.

Consulted: Google Translate: http://translate.google.com/; Tesseract Optical Character Recognition: http://code.google.com/p/tesseract-ocr/

HTML5 REFERENCE GUIDE

Screenshot:

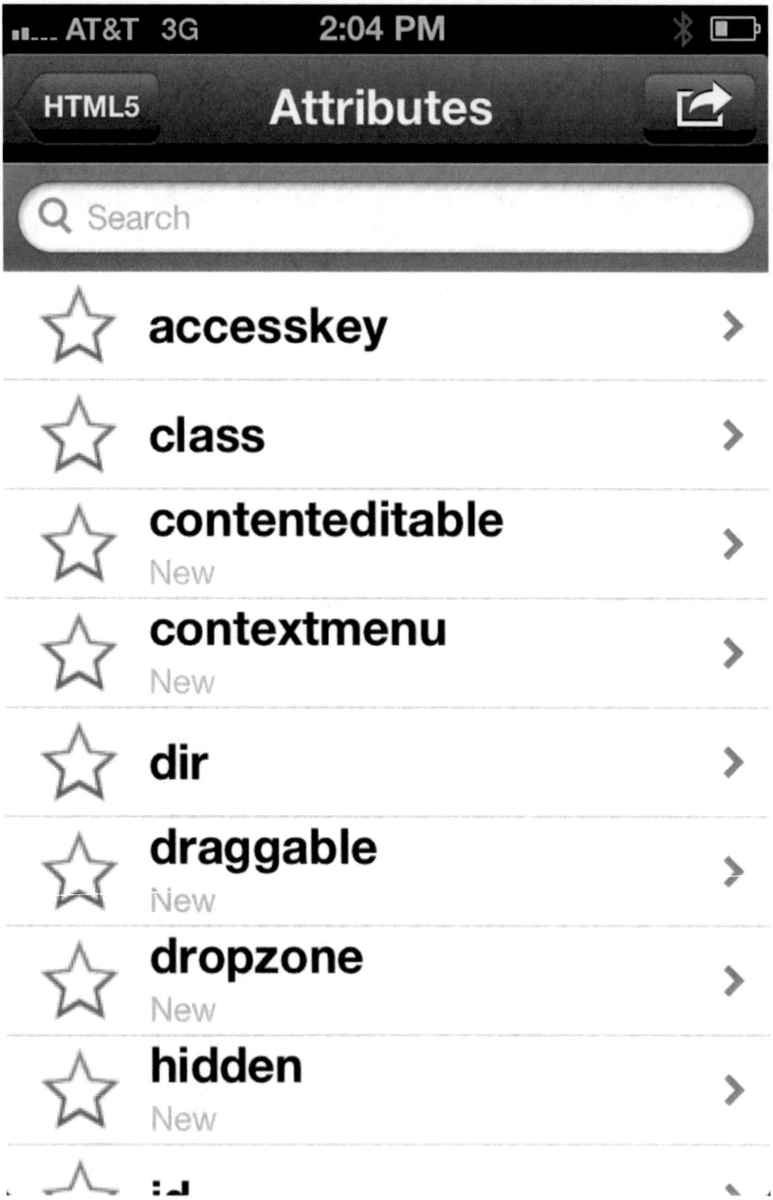

Figure 2.13.   HTML5 Reference Guide. The app will show users an alphabetical list of HTML5 attributes.

What it does: This is a reference source of new and emerging HTML standards. Tags, global attributes, and event attributes are displayed on a first level of the app interface; on the second level of content the elements are organized alphabetically. The reference pages give concise examples of usage and definitions for the HTML5 standard.

Use case: Collection development librarians in the technical and computer science literature will know that traditional reference books that center on online technology are likely to become obsolete within a year. With mobile access to an HTML reference guide librarians could quickly show a novice web developer what various tags and elements mean; HTML5 is an evolving standard, and as it becomes more popular a reference source such as this may actually be more up-to-date than any printed reference guide the library can provide.

Additional use case: An additional use case of the HTML5 reference tool includes reaching out to populations that libraries may not have traditionally served: the technology savvy, who may not have traditionally viewed libraries as being particularly relevant or germane to their life. If a library blog, website, or reference desk is suggesting tools that are tech-focused in nature and which help to supplement the traditional collections, libraries may make inroads to better serving the technical populations of their user communities.

What you should know/more information about how it works: This is a fairly bare bones and streamlined app. While the definitions are concise, without much instructional material, this app works as a reference tool for quick and readily accessible information. It also remains to be seen how up-to-date this app stays, as the HTML5 specification is evolving. It may be updated and added to as time goes on. Note also that this resource is not instructional in nature, and will not necessarily teach anyone who is new to HTML language how to describe web content.

Apps like this to look out for in the future: Future mobile apps that address emerging technology standards will be of great use in library and information settings—these apps point to reference sources, or replace the traditional reference tools. Much like Wikipedia and related blog resources, online tools are extremely well-suited to answer technical questions, and also stay current in offering useful technical reference.

Consulted: https://itunes.apple.com/us/app/id377956033

IBOOKSAPP

Screenshot:

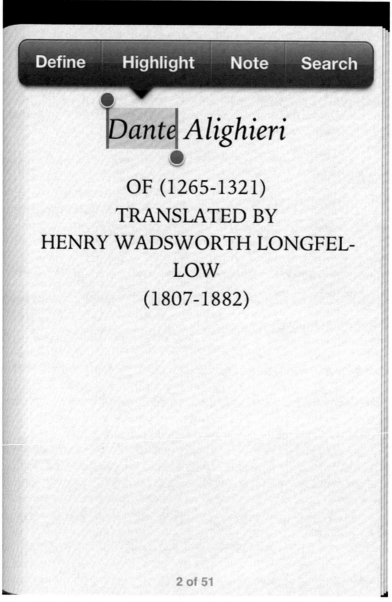

Figure 2.14. iBooks app. Highlighting and selecting words from the text can provide an intelligent reading experience on your mobile device.

What it does: After downloading the iBooks app from the iTunes Store, you'll sense that something is missing—the interface is a blank shelf, a blank wooden shelf. There is much more to this little bookshelf app than an initial glance would reveal. First off, you should know that this app is actually Apple's e-book gateway. A platform inside of an app. How can an app get away with such ambitions? Well, recall that this is Apple's iBook app, and this app provides a gateway to much free reading, kind of like a library.

With this app you can download and access e-books through the iBookstore from your iPhone. You might think that the iPhone or even iPad isn't your preferred medium for e-book reading, and, frankly, libraries haven't quite got the greatest options available. The market is fragmented and siloed and there isn't really one way to get access to every e-book out there. This is one potential gateway into e-books; it shouldn't have to be your only access to e-book content. With this app you can purchase New York Times bestsellers in addition to other books offered by a fairly well-stocked iBookstore. The browsing features you can use include a features tab, charts, search, and purchased.

Features related to app performance include a simple swipe to page forward and a tap of the page to go to the previous page. The app mimics the actual pagination, but again on an iPhone the readability may be less than desirable for lengthy reading. In short increments a user of the app could find reading bits of a paperback to be enjoyable. Which brings us to the use case for this app.

Use case: Consider that you are about to take a flight. You are at the airport and cannot decide what magazine, periodical, or novel would help you through your flight. If you have your iPad or iPhone with you, and you are able to download the iBooks app in the airport, you may find a treasure of available books. You are new to the app but you are able to locate the *Store* button in the upper corner of the app—from here, the iBookstore, you page over to the featured apps—you are reminded of the iTunes Store, and you can navigate around this interface in much the same way. You see the book by that author you always wanted to read but did not have the time for. Since your Apple Store credentials are already loaded you go ahead and download (purchase) the book. It downloads to your bookshelf much the same way an app gets loaded onto your iOS device. Nice, now you have reading for the flight, and you don't have the extra pounds of a lengthy book to carry, either.

(continued)

IBOOKSAPP (*continued*)

Additional use case: Libraries aren't in a position to loan the content of these apps (the book content) out to others. This would be a violation of licensing, so libraries can load the app without content, allowing the user to connect to the iBookstore through the iPhone or iPad and then download e-book content. Since this book is primarily concerned with content that is freely accessible, and libraries are mainly concerned with the broadest access possible, you will want to use the browse tab in the iBookstore and tap the collection of *Top Free Books*. From this part of the iBooks app you can get books without having to make a purchase. In addition a handy feature in the current release of the iBooks app is the ability to download a sample of a book before purchasing. It would be feasible to have many book samples on the iBooks shelf since many users of the app would only be interested in reading a chapter or less at a time on their iPhone. Finally, a use case that libraries may want to explore is to load a library iPad or an iPhone with the sample chapters of any new books the library has recently acquired. In this way, users could read sample chapters, potentially driving traffic or awareness to the recently added print collection in the library.

What you should know/more information about how it works: In the airport example above it is assumed that you are able to get access to network data. Without this you wouldn't be able to get the content of the book. Or another way of saying this is to stress that not all airlines will offer in-fight Internet access, so it will really pay off if you can get your purchases or sample chapters into the app (on your bookshelf) before you get on the plane. Other than that, the app is fairly straightforward. You should know that it isn't compatible with other e-readers—maybe it should be, but at this time the device independence of e-books is not a widely supported paradigm. This is sort of the topic of the next section.

Apps like this to look out for in the future: Will there be anything comparable in the future? There are of course, the other book readers such as the Nook, and of course the Kindle, which has been dominating the market. In the future there may actually be a proliferation of other platforms, so that the field of commercial electronics combined with an evolving marketplace might actually make this domain more complicated, not less, over time. The e-book and e-reader market does find ways to keep their traditional paradigms established. Look for more and varied e-reader book apps in the future. The real hope would be a marketplace that found a balance among author rights to profits and publisher profitability in the context of electronic app access.

Consulted: https://itunes.apple.com/us/app/ibooks/id364709193?mt=8

KEY RING

Screenshot:

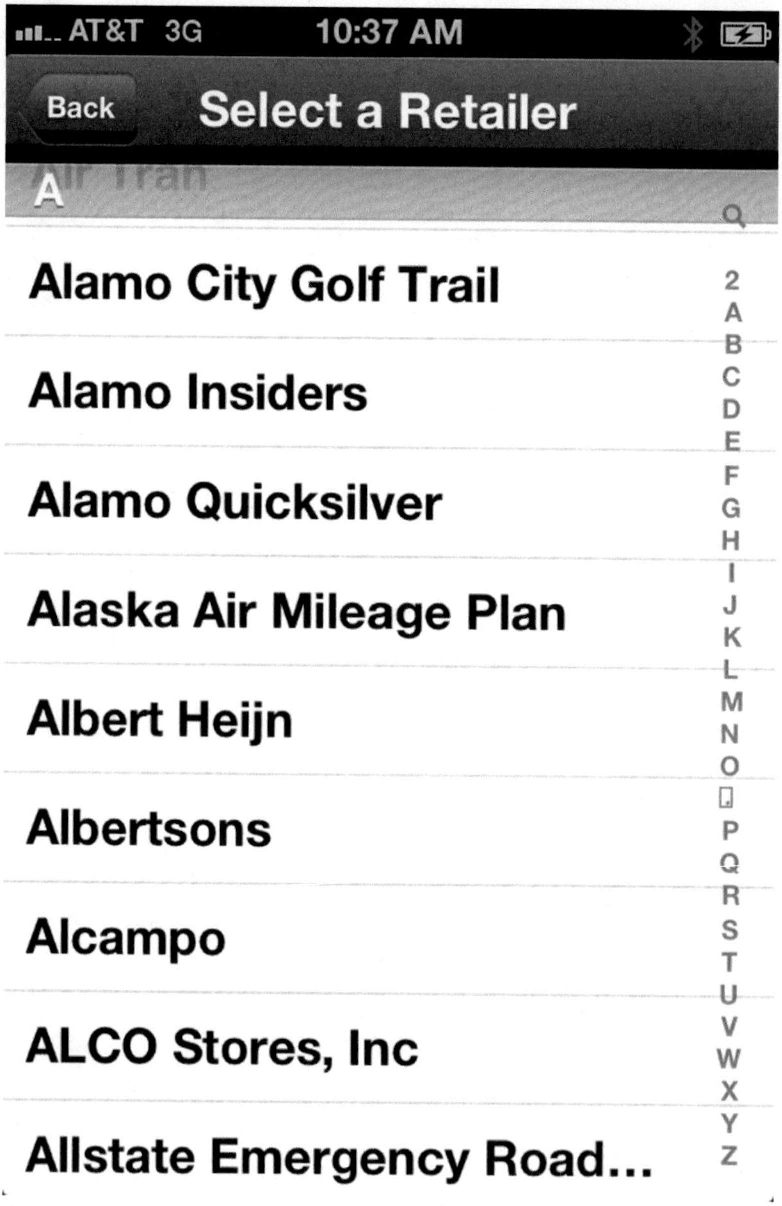

Figure 2.15. Key Ring. The app is pre-loaded with participating retailers that the user can select.

What it does: You can basically store all of your loyalty cards here in one app, meaning you don't have to have all those plastic short cards hanging from your key chain. When you get to the grocery store, all you need to do is show the cashier the scanned barcode and get all the discounts your key ring entitles you to. Another use of course is to store a library barcode here and then use this at the library when you check out books.

Use case: Within the library sphere, patrons could load their library barcode onto this app and use it when checking out books. This would be helpful for patrons who do not carry their library card, or who have simply forgotten to bring their library card with them to the library.

Additional use case: It may be the case that there are staff side uses for holding onto multiple barcode numbers or barcode labels. These may include having barcode control numbers for dummy/fake patrons for testing—and the barcodes may also be useful for testing out equipment. If you have new peripherals that you want to be compliant with app-based barcodes, you may want to load these test barcodes into the app. Additional staff side uses may include checking in materials or checking out periodicals for binding. Storing all of this information in one app may make it easier for staff to process large quantities of binding, or other books that need attention, like repair or other conservation efforts.

What you should know/more information about how it works: One problem users may encounter when trying out this app is that the barcode scanning tool that the library or store owns may not be compatible with reading a scan off a phone. For certain retailers this won't be a problem. However, in the library use case, you want to make sure that your library scanners can accommodate this service since you don't want to recommend something that cannot be used in your facility.

Apps like this to look out for in the future: Apps that act as your barcode are harbingers of a different sort of app—this includes ones that act more like keys than key rings. With the proliferation of near-field communications technology in day-to-day life, you will be able to open your car door and start your vehicle, open the front door to your house, and even use it to get access to an additional array of services like quick checkout, mobile-enhanced payment, and other award-type card processing.

Consulted: http://itunes.apple.com/us/app/key-ring-reward-cards/id372547556?mt=8

MY DATA MANAGER

Screenshot:

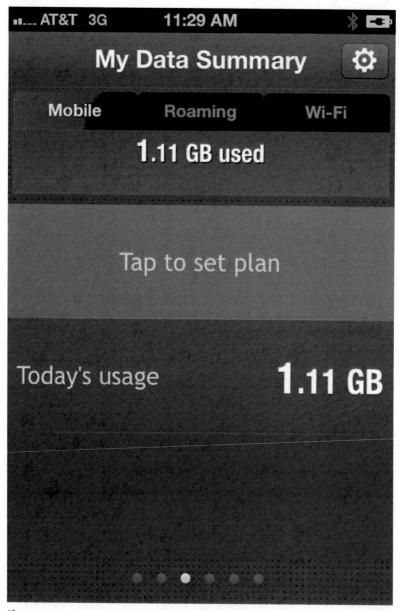

Figure 2.16. My Data Manager. The app can provide you with a usage break down by day.

What it does: The "My Data Manager" app can help you keep track of your monthly data usage. Usually there are overages for certain plans, and the days of unlimited data access are passing from the mobile landscape. Use this app to track which of your apps are using data, and how much data you are using daily. The manager is super helpful since you get to configure how much of an allowance you have in your plan, and when the data plan cycle begins. The app needs to have location settings allowed in order for it to run in the background and provide the detailed data usage information.

Use case: Librarians may want to recommend this app to users who have questions regarding purchasing a data plan. While purchasing the plan can be an important decision, actually managing and tracking your usage is not always straightforward, since it may require logging in to the phone provider's website or learning additional phone functionality. Librarians will most likely be using a device that they can connect to WiFi and so a data plan tracker won't necessarily be used for tracking your subscription usage, but you may want to load the app anyway, as a way of showing the cost savings of getting your data by way of wireless Internet, rather than a subscription data plan—you can also research which of the apps you are using actually use up the most data, if such assessment might be useful when considering mobile tech usage in your library setting.

What you should know/more information about how it works: As I noted above, one peculiar thing you'll notice is that the app will request your location. You do need to enable location services in order to get the full functionality from the app. Also, the app allows you to configure when your data plan begins and ends (the monthly allowances of the plan you have). If you don't know this information or decide not to input it, the app will not be able to keep you from overages. As a result, the app takes a bit of initial outlay to get functioning up to your personalized needs.

Apps like this to look out for in the future: The management of wireless data will depend on carrier plans—if the current trajectory is any indication, we can most likely expect this area to grow in importance. Apps that can send you notifications about benchmarked app usage will be useful and likely leaders in the sphere. Additionally, it may be the case that future designers of apps will make their apps data-light and try to design for a marketplace in which data access can be a costly attribute of mobile computing.

Consulted: http://itunes.apple.com/us/app/my-data-manager/id47786 5384?mt=8

PASSBOOK (IOS)

Screenshot:

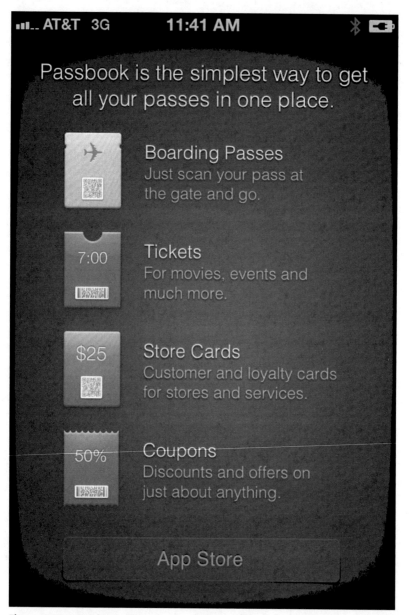

Figure 2.17.   Passbook. There are a number of diverse uses that include tickets and coupons among others.

What it does: The new iPhone OS (iOS 6) comes preloaded with a new native app called Passbook. This mobile application is aimed at the mobile commerce market. You can store a number of different payment and commerce apps within this app, including movie tickets, loyalty cards like Starbucks, and airplane tickets as well. It is a native app, but you will need to load third-party apps into it in order to make use of specific company offers and functionality. Passbook features helpful location services—if you have the Starbucks card loaded into Passbook, the Starbucks reward card will be brought up in your phone's home screen when you walk into a Starbucks store.

Use case: Library services may be positioned to make use of the passbook with some interesting location services as well. When users are near your library, your library app loaded into Passbook could let users know about events going on that day; you could push out event updates just by knowing that the user is within range/proximity on a given day.

Alternative use case: Alternatively, this app could be loaded with other library rewards cards. In the case of summer reading, one way to reach out to the millennial cohort would be to provide awards based on the books or projects young adults are working on during the summer. As a Passbook app, the library may be able to get buy-in from a population that may otherwise be unengaged with library services or collections.

What you should know/more information about how it works: With the advent of iOS 6 developers need to prepare their apps for Passbook integration, so if you are used to making any kind of rewards card available from your phone, check to see if that app is ready for Passbook. It may take some time to get ready, but upon release, American Airlines and Starbucks were already getting set for integration with new versions of their mobile applications. The pervasive mobile commerce arena is seeing a little more innovation with the iPhone 5 and the release of the iOS 6.

Apps like this to look out for in the future: Mobile location services will begin to make inroads in the future. While the mobile landscape for payments is frought with many different players, perhaps Apple can do for mobile payments what it did for music downloads with iTunes—it could offer a business paradigm for the future—or it may lead to some other more innovative application for mobile payments.

Consulted: http://www.apple.com/ios/whats-new/#passbook

PAYPAL

Screenshot:

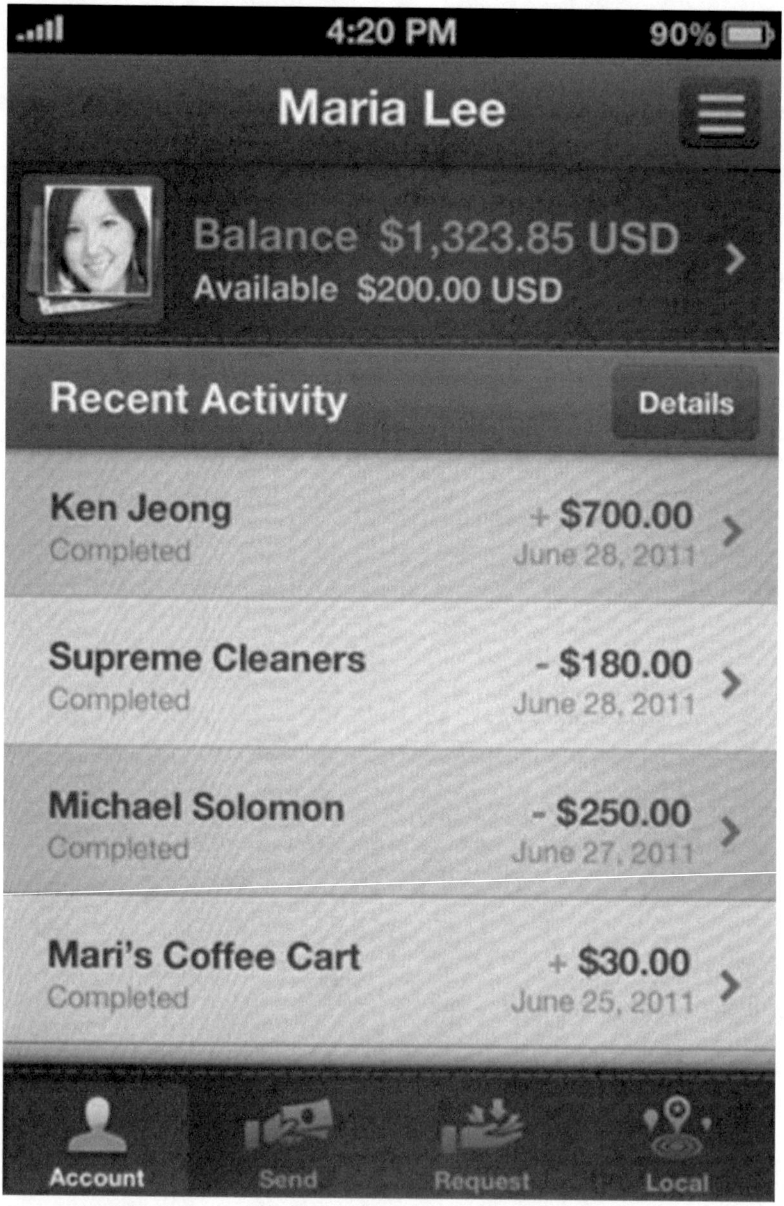

Figure 2.18.   Paypal. A user of the PayPal app can view their current charges on an account.

What it does: This is the mobile interface for the online payment service PayPal. The app is helpful for when you are away from a desktop system and may need a mobile payments solution. With this app, you can send money to individuals from your PayPal account.

Use case: Public service librarians will have observed that a range of commerce needs is supported by public workstations in library settings. These commerce-based activities require users to do a fair amount of paying online. There are a lot of options out there, but one of the most popular payment processing tools is PayPal, especially for your library patrons that are working in or running small businesses. A software solution that can help them process payments makes sense for users who may not have access to desktop-based computing, or for when users are away from desktop resources.

What you should know/more information about how it works: This app will ask for your current location. Also, one thing about using PayPal through a mobile interface—you will want to have set up your account and billing information previously, since doing this on the go may not be possible depending on your situation, need, and circumstances.

Apps like this to look out for in the future: Payments on the web are going to go the way of mobile. This is a sphere that is poised to expand over time. Watch for deeper integration of your phone's hardware with mobile payment options. This includes things like near-field communication and other infrastructure-based payments.

Consulted: https://itunes.apple.com/us/app/paypal/id283646709?mt=8

PDANET (ANDROID)

Screenshot:

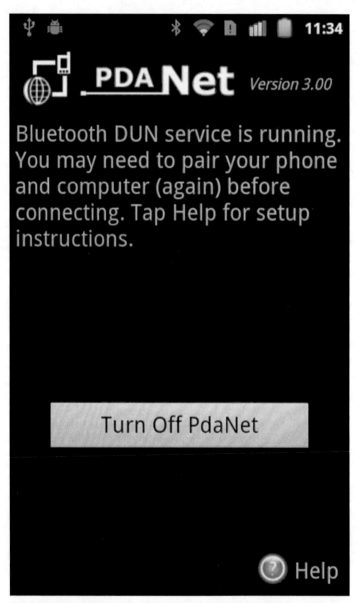

Figure 2.19. PdaNet. The first step of accessing WiFi through your Android device is to pair your phone with your computer while the PdaNet client is running on the computer.

What it does: This software helps you connect your laptop to the Internet by creating a WiFi access point from your phone. You have three options to connect: USB Tether Mode, Bluetooth DUN Mode, or WiFi Hotspot Mode. Your phone, with its data access plan, already has Internet connectivity, but this specific software allows you to share that Internet access by broadcasting your phone as an access point. There is an additional third-party tool for the WiFi Hotspot Mode that PdaNet will connect you with for functionality.

Use case: Librarians who work in embedded roles or offsite from traditional library infrastructures may have a laptop that they carry with them, but they may be in a building where WiFi may not be available, or they may not have credentials to make use of the WiFi network. With the PdaNet application, librarians can get a Bluetooth connection established between their laptop and an Android phone that has the PdaNet software loaded on it.

Additional use case: Additionally, for conference-going librarians, access to Internet connectivity on the go, especially in conference areas, can be problematic and troublesome to navigate. The PdaNet app is a helpful backup for when your conference either doesn't offer WiFi or the WiFi requires prohibitively expensive credentials.

What you should know/more information about how it works: The PdaNet app is currently not available for iOS devices. Recent iOS releases have included native functionality for creating a personal WiFi hotspot from your phone's Internet connection.

Apps like this to look out for in the future: Since data needs for library services, particularly mobile data needs, are likely to grow over time, a service that allows you to create your own WiFi access points on demand is valuable. Apps in this domain are difficult to predict since they exist at the intersection of what mobile carriers allow and what manufacturers design.

Consulted: https://play.google.com/store/apps/details?id=com.pn.helper

PODCASTS (IOS)

Screenshot:

Figure 2.20.   Podcasts. There are numerous podcast stations a user of this app can browse. Indicated above is one of the educational language course stations.

What it does: The Podcasts iOS app is a new app from Apple that helps you organize and subscribe to podcast content. The app is not just for organizing content, since you are also able to expand your podcast library by searching through the iTunes-provided podcasts—you can search by category, or, if you prefer, you can search by top podcasts stations. The app offers functionality that allows you to sync with content that is in your iTunes podcast library.

Use case: Consider a library staff with a shared iTunes library. This iTunes library is seeded with content and videos that would help the librarians stay up-to-date and current in various fields. It may have a diverse range of perspectives and content available. The librarians and other staff who rely on this iTunes library may find it cumbersome or otherwise troubling to keep track of what podcasts they have listened to, and what to subscribe to next. This may be particularly troubling in the case of librarians who are trying to listen to the content from a mobile device that has been synced with the iTunes account. Rather than trying to get all of your content organized and up-to-date from a shared staff workstation, it may make sense to actually use the Podcast app for all your sharing, listening, accessing, and searching of streaming library content.

Additional use case: An additional use case for this application is for language learning. If you search through the video content of the podcasts you will be able to locate an education category. In this category there are multiple language courses available. By selecting the language-learning course that you desire you can get updated video content for supplementing any second language that you or patrons are currently studying. This would be a particularly useful app for students in their first year of college; it has been a finding in focus groups that the mobile apps the first-year students are interested in locating and using are the ones that could support them in the first semester and first year of language learning courses.

What you should know/more information about how it works: Users can also enjoy podcast video content subscriptions from the Podcast app as well. As an additional use case you do have the opportunity in the app to share your favorite podcast episodes by way of Twitter or email.

Apps like this to look out for in the future: This app replicates the podcast discovery functionality of the iTunes Store. It may be the case that apps like this in the future will actually provide a deeper replication or emulation of functionalities that users have come to expect from the iTunes Store.

Consulted: https://itunes.apple.com/us/app/podcasts/id525463029?mt=8

QR READER FOR IPHONE

Screenshot:

Figure 2.21. QR Reader for iPhone. The user of the app is able to create QR codes in addition to scanning QR codes.

What it does: This is a QR code reader for the iPhone. This QR code reader starts up in scan mode so that you can quickly find the linked information embedded in a 2-d code. By default the app retains images of your scans so you can go back over your history of previous scans and find past links and resources that you may want to go over again. The app also features social network integration so that you can share scans/links and resources by way of your Facebook timeline or Twitter feed. You are able to create your own QR codes from this app as well.

Use case: There are multiple uses for QR code generation in library settings. Some libraries have gone so far as to create a QR code for every item in their collection, but this is just another way of bringing library users back to their online catalog, or drawing emerging technologies into the bibliographic sphere. But that doesn't have to be the case—librarians can actually bring users to dynamic media content that relates to specific installations or displays from within the library. The QR code at places in the library allows users to connect a physical location with digital media—you might consider integrating helpful and instructive videos in areas of the library where patrons are likely to encounter problems or have frequently asked questions.

What you should know/more information about how it works: The app does have a QR code creator, which many library users may not think to make use of on the fly. If librarians get questions about how to create QR codes, designing one from inside of this app may be a possible suggestion for patrons and other library users.

Apps like this to look out for in the future: QR codes are becoming increasingly popular. Also, many apps that scan barcodes are making use of third-party code to do this as a part of their software—look for QR code scanning to become more integrated into other apps in the future.

Consulted: https://itunes.apple.com/us/app/qr-reader-for-iphone/id36 8494609?mt=8

QUICK PERIODIC TABLE OF THE ELEMENTS

Screenshot:

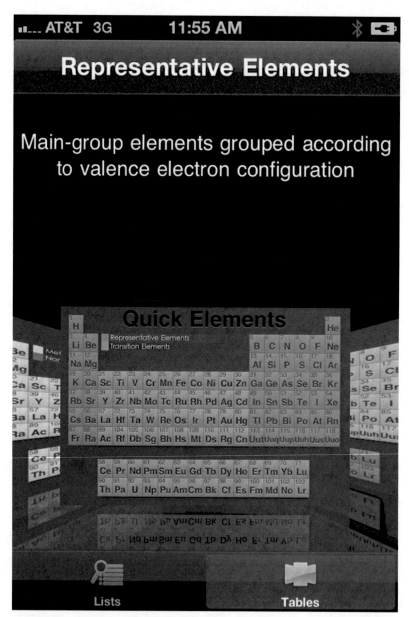

Figure 2.22.   Quick Periodic Table of the Elements. The view representation above is the main-group elements grouped according to valence electron configuration.

What it does: This is a reference for the periodic table of elements. The app supports multiple views of the periodic table. The first load of the app lets you choose by either table view or list view. The list view allows you to search for elements by name or by symbol. The interface of the table view is organized by chemical categories, class (metals, non-metals, and metalloids), representative elements, and orbital blocks.

Use case: A good use case of the Quick Periodical Table of the Elements would be to re-envision this app as a concise, ready reference tool. With an easy chemistry reference tool such as this, students can pan through element information in a visually interactive and engaging way. Students in the undergraduate sphere may actually find this way of engaging with chemistry material to be more relevant to their digital experiences.

Additional use case: Alternatively a tool like this could be used to introduce basic science concepts to younger learners such as those in middle school, or those in high school that are learning the foundations of molecules or chemistry for the first time.

What you should know/more information about how it works: This app is functionally not too complicated; its information is fairly well organized and presented, though those with greater knowledge of science principles will be able to navigate all the views more expertly than novice science users.

Apps like this to look out for in the future: It may be the case that in the future more of the chemistry or general science learning apps may lend themselves to graphical manipulation and interaction like augmented reality overlays. Augmented reality simply means the graphical overlay of information over real world objects—so students might find science applications compelling and interesting in this realm.

Consulted: https://itunes.apple.com/us/app/quick-periodic-table-ele ments/id467937518?mt=8

QUICK SCAN

Screenshot:

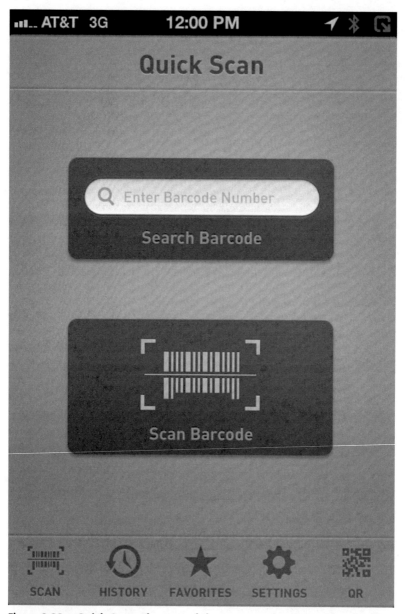

Figure 2.23. Quick Scan. The user of the app can choose to either key in a barcode manually, or make use of the camera on the mobile device for scanning.

What it does: The Quick Scan app is a basic barcode scanner—scan a book in a bookstore or library and it will connect you to online booksellers—it can display price information so you can decide if the price in the store or online would be a better deal. In the basic version, the QR code scanner is not enabled—you must upgrade to the paid version in order to use the barcode scan as well as the QR code scan.

Use case: In the library stacks, users will desire to connect to digital content. This app makes it possible to help users understand the digital associations with the print book stacks. Does a user want to make a purchase of a reference encyclopedia or perhaps a DVD that he did not know existed? An app such as this can connect the library user to an online retailer for making such a purchase.

Additional use case: Users that want to build up a possible reading list can collect scanned barcodes into the history module/component of the app; from here, a list of the items that the readers wanted to consult later will be available. This may be useful for users to keep track of the sections of the library they passed through, or the subject areas that were of interest—the Quick Scan app can give users a listing of their thought process or topical search path over the course of scanning these items.

What you should know/more information about how it works: The app works by finding the ISBN number and searching its database for sellers who have indexed this ISBN in their database. When an ISBN a library patron searches for does not come up in the app, this does not necessarily mean that the item is not for sale online or that it cannot be purchased anywhere—this may just indicate a missing ISBN from the backend infrastructure of the Quick Scan app. This app can use your location for information delivery. At the same time, it also uses the push notification to send information. You can choose to enable or disable these settings.

Apps like this to look out for in the future: Vision search with cameras on a smartphone is an area ripe for innovation—it may even translate into other wearable interfaces, like the highly anticipated Google Glasses that are making their way to market.

Consulted: http://itunes.apple.com/us/app/quick-scan-barcode-scanner/id446067710?mt=8

SHAZAM

Screenshot:

Figure 2.24.   Shazam. The interface allows the user for one-touch identification of songs that are currently playing.

What it does: This app will identify the title of a song as it is playing. Simply activate the app when the song is playing, hold the phone to the speaker and the app will match the features of the song against its database. If the song is in Shazam's database, then it will provide the user with the title of the song and the user will also have the option to download or purchase the song from an online music source.

Use case: Librarians are sometimes faced with identifying novels or short stories simply based on the patron's synopsis of a plot. Sometimes the librarians are able to use this information to identify the book, if it is widely known, but other times, simply knowing the plot is not enough. Songs, too, may be a requested item to identify, and if the librarian tries the common usage of Google's autosuggestion feature for song lyrics and doesn't come up with the song, an app like Shazam would be very useful. The app could even be used to remember the songs that you like, since Shazam also comes loaded with a "history" feature.

Additional use case: Users may also be interested in sharing their identified song titles with others. The Shazam app therefore also includes Facebook integration—you can publish all your Shazam activities to your Facebook timeline. What this means is that when you would identify a song and then tag it as something new that you enjoy listening to, the app would push this notification out to your Facebook profile. In order to enable this you simply log in with your Facebook credentials and the app will handle the rest of the data sharing. Facebook's Open Graph protocol uses structured data that does the magic of connecting the relevant data with your timeline.

What you should know/more information about how it works: This application does require a data connection in order to do song matching, so an offline mode is not possible with Shazam. The underlying architecture for music identification requires a sample of music that it then attempts to match, but you need to get a decent sample, so getting close to the speakers or source of the music will help greatly to accomplish the matching. Finally, if the song is rare, unique, or very new even, the matching may not work since there may not be an adequate sample in existence in the Shazam servers.

Apps like this to look out for in the future: Video identification and other search-by-media tools will be an interesting development in the future. These apps will be able to use the video or voice input to find related information and most likely will be driven by commerce, so expect the search-by-media feature to drive traffic to online shopping and other e-commerce sites.

Consulted: https://play.google.com/store/apps/details?id=com.shazam.android

SPEEDTEST.NET

Screenshot:

Figure 2.25.   Speedtest.net. In order to identify the speed of your Internet connection the service first needs to locate a computer (server) nearby to test against.

What it does: This app is the mobile version of the popular online tool Speedtest.net—a resource that allows you to check your data connection speeds with upload and download speed tests. The app includes functionality for historical speed test checks by comparing how your current speeds look against past speed tests. The app also allows users to share their current speed tests with others—you can email the results of speed tests to yourself or other interested parties.

Use case: There may be library resources that users are trying to download at a distance. In the case of a library user facing connectivity issues for downloading articles, data from the library, or other resources, you can ask them to check their connectivity—including uploading and downloading speeds——from this app. It isn't simple from the phone to get a quick view of your IP ranges, but the settings tab from this app can tell you your internal and external IP addresses, which can be useful for troubleshooting connections to library resources.

Additional use case: Alternatively, if users are concerned generally that they don't have any kind of connectivity this app can tell them fairly quickly what type of connection they do have and if the WiFi access point they are connected to is the culprit or if their phone is slow.

What you should know/more information about how it works: This app works in a way similar to the desktop version—in order for you to connect to the test database it figures out your location and then finds test servers near you to optimally give a measure of data performance.

Apps like this to look out for in the future: Testing data speeds seems appropriate to desktop uses mostly. But as more mobile devices begin to be designed like desktops and vice versa, apps like this will become more common— and perhaps make more sense in a tablet-like environment.

Consulted: https://play.google.com/store/apps/details?id=org.zwanoo .android.speedtest

STUMBLEUPON

Screenshot:

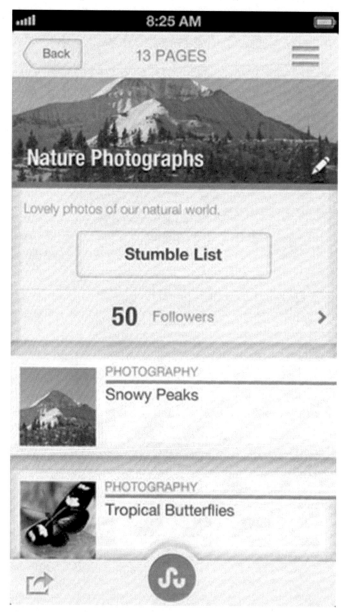

Figure 2.26. StumbleUpon. The app interface offers a visually appealing discovery experience.

What it does: This app is the mobile version of the popular web-sharing service and toolbar. The desktop version of StumbleUpon within desktop-based browsers allows you to share interesting parts of the web with others; with the mobile version the user simply enters in topic of interest and the mobile app will identify things on the web that are interesting based on profiled interests. The app comes with an explanatory introductory overlay so that users will discover pages and interests related to favorite topics quickly and easily.

Use case: Library patrons who are searching for the next read, browsing the Internet, or in need of a topic to research can use this app for information discovery. This mobile research tool can help users explore visually and discover pages of interest. The app features integration with your Facebook account so you are able to log in from your Facebook login, or you can access the mobile interface through your Google credentials as well.

What you should know/more information about how it works: The app features a smart searching algorithm such that for those parts of the app for which you do not record a like and swipe away, the program will learn about your dislikes and start suggesting things that are more interesting to you. With additional use the recommendations should improve over time. Note also that with such personalization features you would want to make sure not to share an account, since the combined recommendations of more than one user may not support the individualized suggestions.

Apps like this to look out for in the future: Future apps in the realm of personalized information discovery will include features like learning/intelligence search support. As an additional feature of apps like this in the future, expect to see a visually compelling search. This will grow in importance as tablet browsing makes visual information more engaging and a more compelling experience for discovery.

Consulted: https://itunes.apple.com/app/stumbleupon/id386244833

SWIFTKEY (ANDROID)

Screenshot:

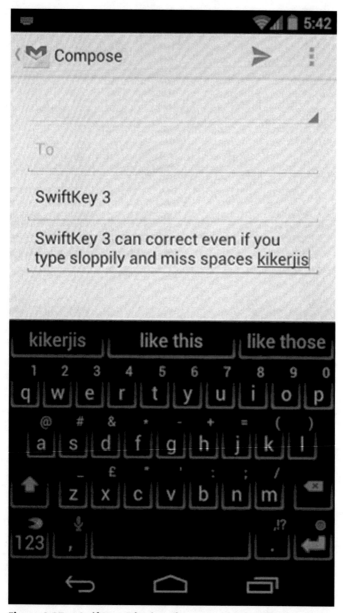

**Figure 2.27.   SwiftKey.   The interface provides intelligent sugges-
tions based on natural language processes.**

What it does: This app is currently only available for Android devices. It offers more efficient predictive typing. This app will help those mobile app users who find the current keyboard autocompletion tools to be cumbersome and incorrect.

Use case: This app is for those library users who cannot use the keyboard, or can only make limited use of current Android keyboard functions. The app is more powerful than current word-completion technologies since it is coded to understand how words fit together in sentences.

What you should know/more information about how it works: The app is built with machine-learning tools so that it learns about the way you type and form sentences as you use the app.

Apps like this to look out for in the future: Future apps in this vein may introduce additional learning and smart/intelligent algorithms to learn globally what functionalities you will need from specific apps throughout the day, or situation, or by location.

Consulted: http://www.swiftkey.net/

WEATHER CHANNEL

Screenshot:

Figure 2.28.   Weather Channel. The mobile app includes a well-designed interface providing essential weather data for the user's location.

What it does: The informative and up-to-date content of the web-based Weather Channel site is encompassed by the mobile application. The tabs of the compressed Weather Channel app include a weather map of your location, a second tab that includes video feeds of content from the weather channel (these are the so-called must-see videos), and then the central tab, which is a forecast of conditions by hour, thirty-six hours, or ten days. The Weather Channel app also pulls in tweets from your area that are weather-related. The user can filter these incoming tweets by location, either selecting nearby tweets or regional tweets. The final tab on the app is the "In Season" tab, indicating various tropical or pollen threats and updates. The tropic weather can be sorted by Atlantic or Tropical timelines.

Use case: Once you find an app like this that provides quick views of information, it becomes one that you will go back to again and again. This is an app you will want to recommend to library patrons for serving up quick up-to-date weather and forecasting information.

Additional use case: Alternatively, having a staff-side, librarian-based application that you can refer to in the case of extreme weather or weather alerts can help to alert patrons if weather conditions require taking cover or otherwise becoming alert—like tornado watches or tornado warnings. This could be particularly useful in certain more alternating weather regions during certain times of the year.

What you should know/more information about how it works: Location and push notifications are available for this app. For this weather app the location feature can give you detailed weather information at your currently detected location. Push notifications can be configured in the weather application settings. The 5.0 version of the app allows you to enable Pollen Push alerts so that information on pollen alerts can be quickly delivered to your phone.

Apps like this to look out for in the future: Popular informational websites are looking to make the move to mobile. Certainly many already have and are looking at the following feature set as they make this transition. It includes social possibilities—pulling in Twitter feeds, the websites continue to offer their core services, providing the feeds and up-to-date information that made them popular in the first place. Finally, these apps, for better or worse, are seeking to leverage two key areas of the mobile computing app development domain—using your location and sending you push notifications. These are part of the framework, and some mobile apps do find good uses for these frameworks, while others are not quite sure what to make of this feature set.

Consulted: http://itunes.apple.com/us/app/the-weather-channel/id295646461?mt=8

XE CURRENCY

Screenshot:

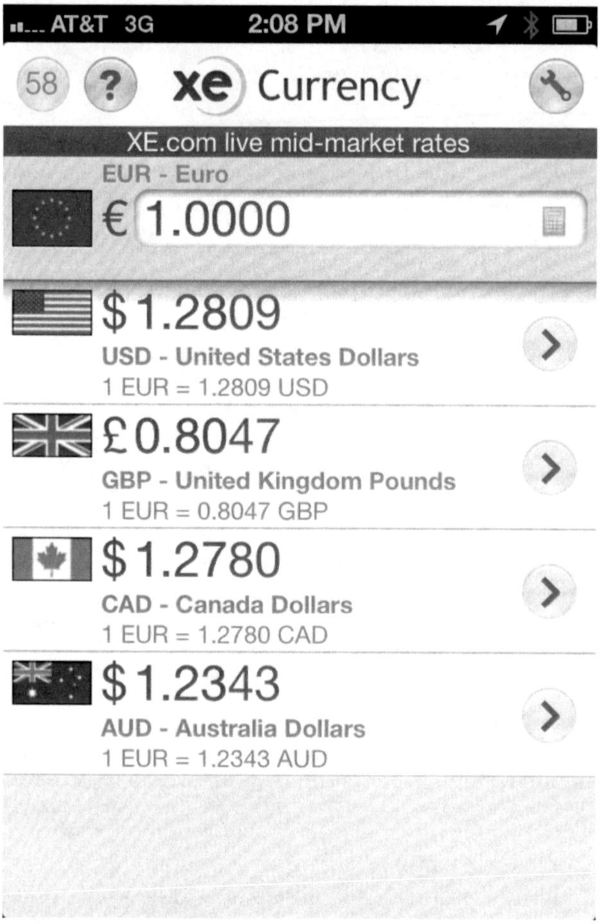

**Figure 2.29.   XE Currency. The user can add multiple curren-
cies to convert in the main view of the interface.**

What it does: This mobile app helps you to convert currency (and prices)
from "every world currency"—an indispensible tool for world travelers, especially those who will find themselves in areas with different or
unique currency. The latest rates get loaded every minute, so it is up-to-
date. If you find yourself in an area without Internet access, then you
will still be able to get currency converted by the app, which will use the
last-loaded rate—so as long as the last loaded rate is not years old, you
should be able to obtain a fairly accurate conversion. The app also uses

your location—the location settings don't actually help you to convert currency, but rather it sends your data back to a currency map mash-up page, where the data on recently made conversions are presented.

Use case: Librarians may want to suggest this app in tandem with other currency-converter tools. Certainly a Google computation can do the conversion, but if a user is mobile or does not have Internet access immediately available, this app can be recommended to the user as a means to still get currency converted in new countries or locations where data access cannot be guaranteed.

Additional use case: This may be useful for certain business applications—if you are on a campus or in an academic library and involved in information literacy instruction, there may be lessons you can impart that are related to critical thinking skills and evaluating information. Consider a lesson on how to know you need information: you are at an airport, and you are wondering if converting your currency here is the best option for you—teaching students with this scenario will get them thinking about finding and evaluating information in their setting.

What you should know/more information about how it works: The app uses some functions of being a phone that help to make it easier to access data, for example, resetting the base currency back to 1.00 as a new query point is as easy as shaking the phone—which is an intuitive process if you are accustomed to using mobile apps—otherwise you just shake the phone and watch as the base currency changes. It is magical. You should also know your data is getting (theoretically) logged by the app if you are enabling location sharing. It seems off a bit if your mobile app is sending your data back to a mash-up but not actually doing any location services when you enable location sharing.

Apps like this to look out for in the future: The kind of innovation you may see for this type of utility app may be related to predictive analytics—i.e., data-mining tools that will tell you if you should purchase a currency now, or if, by waiting another day or two, you can get a better deal on that large Euro purchase you are about to make. Such predicative tools currently exist for flights (Farecast, at Bing, is one such example). The historic rates can be a supplemental source of information and potentially useful for this purpose.

Consulted: http://www.xe.com/apps/iphone/

Chapter 3

Augmented Reality Apps for Library Services

When we talk of immersive apps we talk about those mobile applications that have roots in the gaming side of app design; these immersive apps can also incorporate aspects of augmented reality. Augmented reality apps may seem space-age and perhaps too bleeding edge tech for the beginner. They are not so complicated, really.

What an augmented reality application does, essentially, is to overlay graphics onto the phone's camera in real time. It uses computer vision technology to map out the geometry of the scene and affixes graphics to it. Now, the very interesting thing for libraries is that these graphics can incorporate information—library information—into the environment.

The immersive application could be used in a library setting for animated wayfinding or even with augmented reality applications. One practical use would be in locating specific sections of the library stacks with a navigation app. That area represents some further research and development. For those who want to track development here, there are ongoing conferences and conference proceedings from the International Symposium on Mixed and Augmented Reality, http://ismar.vgtc.org/.

GOOGLE SKY MAP (ANDROID)

Screenshot:

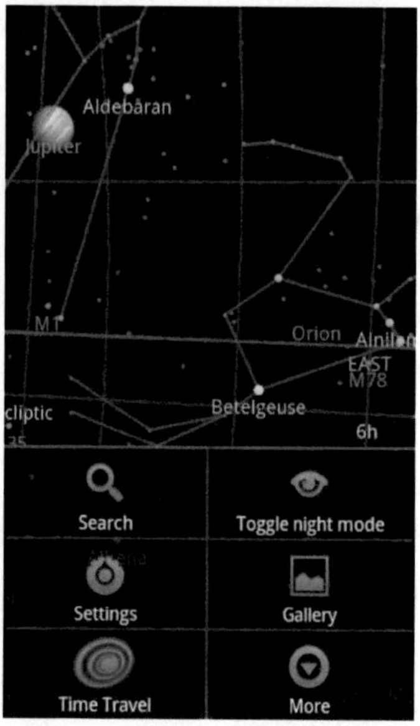

Figure 3.1. Google Sky Map. There are many value-added features built into the Sky Map than would appear at first glance. See, for example, the menu options at the bottom of the interface.

What it does: Google Sky Map is a reference source for identifying constellations and stars. This app is that combination of hardware (gyroscope and compass) with software (constellation data) that creates a compelling and even somewhat magical experience for providing users information based on location and needs. When you tap the Google Sky app and point it at the sky, it will identify constellations by name and also show you how they appear. Since, to the novice night sky gazer, it may seem that we are only seeing parts of constellations, or partial views of the night sky depending on conditions, this handy application will help you to verify that the constellation that you are looking at truly is the constellation you have identified it to be.

Use case: Consider the library patron that is consulting star charts about constellations or other types of astronomy information. If the library patron is interested in this information in the context of stargazing it makes sense to suggest the Google Sky app for that situation. Not all librarians will be familiar with the Android service of Google Sky Map, but the gist of it is that the user points his or her device at the sky and then the star charts are presented in real time, depending on where the phone is pointed. If you point the phone away from the horizon, directly at the ground, you will get the charts for the other side of the globe, as if the phone is "seeing" through the earth to the other parallel horizon.

Additional use case: There are two modes, manual and automatic. The automatic mode will just tell you what the phone is pointing at. However, if you put the Google Sky app into the manual mode, you will be able to scroll around manually, across all charts.

What you should know/more information about how it works: The panel on the side of the app viewfinder is a series of layers that allows you to filter to show the following: stars, constellations, Messier objects, planets, meteor showers, RA/Dec. grid, and horizon. These options are not clearly explained inside of the app, however, the options menu will provide textual information on what the icons stand for. Some more intuitive indication of the buttons would be desirable, since the icons aren't clearly indicating functionality.

For any Android application you will want to inspect the menu/options button on the phone, and see what other functionalities are built into the app. The menu button is (usually) on the actual hardware of the phone itself, and clicking the menu/options allows you to see additional options that may not be on the screen/interface of the first-level page for the app. For the Sky Map app, there are some very interesting features that you will want to explore; for example, there is an available search module where you can search for a planet or star by name, a night mode toggle, settings of the app, gallery, and time travel. The time travel function allows the user to jump back to see astrologically significant dates, such as the Apollo Landing, or, say, a solar eclipse in 1919. The gallery, "Sky Map Hubble Gallery," is a beautiful area for images of galaxies, nebulae, and planets, and can guide the users to the phenomena in the sky, as well.

The Google Play website for the app indicates that the data is opened sourced. This is a move by Google to allow its development to be shaped by developers outside of Google, perhaps educators as well as hobbyists. They have a space on Google Plus: http://goo.gl/XWjRg, as well as a Twitter space here: @skymapdevs.

Apps like this to look out for in the future: This app is almost one of a kind. Yet the innovators at Google will most likely find ways to top this in the future. It may be the case that Sky Map data isn't a growth area for the company, which may have fed into the reason why they decided to open source it to a community of developers.

What Google may use this type of data interaction to overlay street directions onto their prototypes of Google Glasses or perhaps see integration into the Google Car's overhead display; the reference sources of street or map data may help users identify buildings, streets, or other areas of interest with navigation needs.

Consulted: https://play.google.com/store/apps/details?id=com.google.android.stardroid

LAYAR REALITY BROWSER

Screenshot:

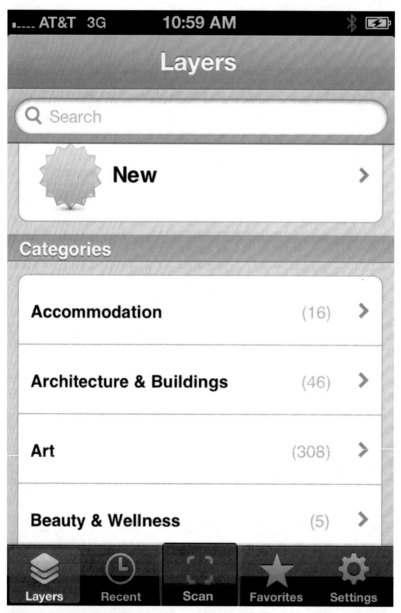

Figure 3.2.   Layar Reality Browser. There are a number of category types for which augmented reality overlays are available.

What it does: This app overlays dynamic information onto your phone's camera view so that you can learn more information about your surrounding environment. Through a series of layers, the user is able to specify what types of information are of interest in the surrounding environment.

Use case: First-time visitors to your library will only be aware of print objects that the library has available. However, librarians subscribe to an array of digital resources. Some users may actually prefer an e-book to the print copy if available. With the Layar SDK, librarians are able to specify available digital content based on the library user's location. Since much of the digital library content could be association with a geographic location, the library could bring digital content into the user's everyday urban navigation experience.

Additional use case: For new members of your patron population, the librarian at the reference desk may want to recommend this app for exploring their new city. Users can specify to receive information about food, housing, shopping, and a number of other social functions as well.

What you should know/more information about how it works: This app uses the phone's positioning sensors to approximate the device location. Users should be aware that their current location will be used in order to deliver localized information. Some mobile users are not comfortable with location sharing. This is an important consideration when making a recommendation for an app. In most use cases, the mobile app will notify the user (basically ask for permission) before utilizing the GPS coordinates on the device. Users have the ability to decline and not make use of location-enabled services.

Apps like this to look out for in the future: Immersive augmented reality applications will have an impact in the realm of gaming. Immersive gaming environments are relevant to library services, since these types of environments will start to influence the expectations users have for locating information and accessing digital content that is geo-referenced with physical objects. Such information-rich overlays could leverage the digitized content that many libraries and cultural institutions already steward; this data re-use will make any library a highly relevant and sought-after partner in augmented reality content delivery.

Consulted: http://www.layar.com

REDLASER APP

Screenshot:

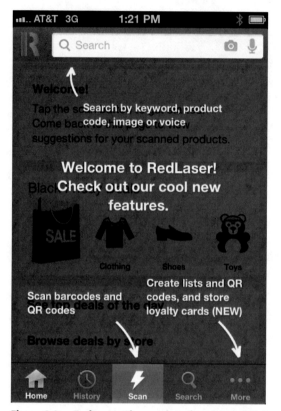

Figure 3.3.   RedLaser. The app interface has helpful first-time-user instructional overlays.

What it does: RedLaser is a barcode-scanning app. Users can scan the barcode of any book using the phone's camera to learn what libraries nearby have this book in their collection.

This app can also be used for price comparison. Simply scan an item in a store and the app will tell the user nearby stores that offer the best price on the item. Works for QR codes, too.

Use case: Librarians at conferences will be bombarded by the popularity of the QR code, and not just librarian conferences; anywhere you have a scientific gathering for sharing research and networking you can expect to see QR codes linking presentations, posters, and whitepapers to online content. The next few years will also see QR codes becoming a standard feature for business cards. Don't ignore the QR code on a business card; you may be inadvertently ignoring the digital components of the individual's work. Scan that QR code with the RedLaser app, which will direct you to their online portfolio.

For the daring systems librarian, RedLaser offers a free Software Developer Kit (SDK): http://redlaser.com/sdk/index.php. The SDK allows you to invent uses within your library environment. This SDK is a powerful entre into the world of location-based services that deliver relevant information based on scanned barcode. Search-by-media will be an important trend for the future mobile information seeker.

Alternative use case: A new college student is in the throes of procrastinating purchasing her new textbooks; she's new to campus and doesn't know where to get books cheaply. The student has previously downloaded the RedLaser app to her phone, which she used to compare prices for clothing purchases. On a whim she considers scanning the barcodes of her roommate's books. RedLaser suggests locations of booksellers around campus that offer competitively priced books; the new student even sees her campus library listed among the search results—something the student had not expected.

What you should know/more information about how it works: Note the intersection of the library in the wider range of consumer-based resources. While information seeking is not always situated in the paradigm of commerce, this app can certainly save your library patrons money and time.

This app searches Google and other data providers for ISBN matches. The makers of RedLaser state that if the item is not indexed in product databases, the app will not function properly. This should temper and manage your users' expectations for what the app can realistically provide.

Apps like this to look out for in the future: In the future your users will most likely want to scan books in the library, either as self-checkout, or as a means to query other relevant information on this topic. Additionally, apps are now reaching consumers that allow them to store barcodes (i.e., library card data) on their phones. Library barcode scanners may need to be updated so that they can parse the information displayed from the phone. Keep in mind not all scanners in operation today will be able to support a scan from the smartphone screen. In this way some apps and phones are disruptive technologies to everyday library workflow.

Consulted: http://support.redlaser.com/discussion/303/RedLaser-App-FAQ

WIKITUDE WORLD BROWSER

Screenshot:

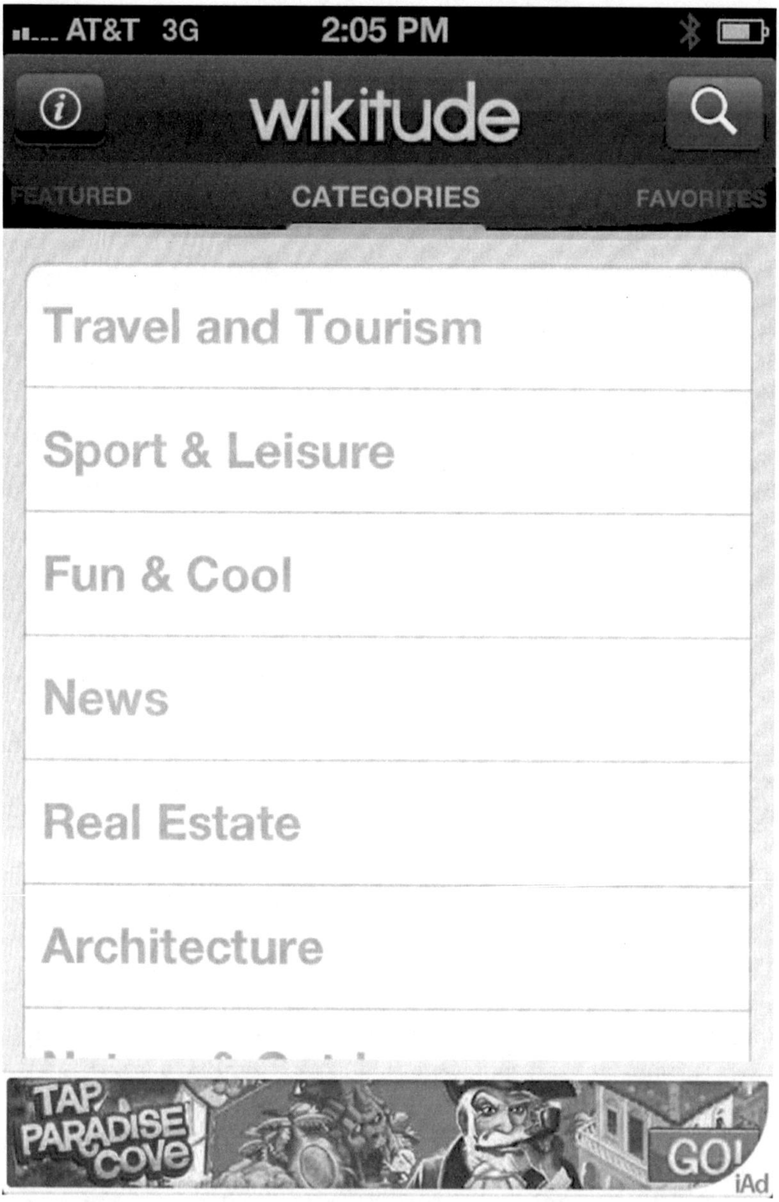

Figure 3.4. Wikitude World Browser. There are numerous and broad categories to choose from for information overlays.

What it does: Described as an augmented reality browser, the application is similar in feature set to the Layar example. It overlays graphical geo-referenced information into the surrounding landscape. The user browses the surrounding geo-referenced information through their camera video feed.

Use case: Traditional libraries and Wikipedia have a storied history. This checkered relationship need not negatively impact the viability of an app like Wikitude. Wikitude isn't just about Wikipedia data overlaid through your smartphone's video feed; it can also overlay any number of information-providing resources, such as Twitter feeds, YouTube content, and Flickr. Of course, the ability to represent these objects requires the back-end metadata to include geo-referenced data such that it can be overlaid onto the real world (3-D object).

Additional use case: Librarians in metropolitan areas may consider making use of the API to add a world browser. Metropolitan areas have buildings that are next to one another and which could help to simulate a true augmented reality kind of experience. To be a true augmented reality application the app is required to affix graphics onto the real world in real time. However, applications like Layar and Wikitude World Browser have not achieved a true mobile augmented reality experience.

What you should know/more information about how it works: Contributed user content makes this app a sort of unknown in terms of quality. There may be gaming uses for library orientation or explorations, and so exploring the SDK would be a wise choice for any intrepid librarian. The Wikitude website describes the Wikitude Browser as its own kind of app store, but it doesn't quite represent the ability to freely develop the way an app store can. If you do create elements for Wikitude, you still do so within the application framework.

Apps like this to look out for in the future: Wikitude calls these geographic overlays "worlds"—similar in concept to the Layar conceptualization of layering your camera input with data.

Consulted: http://www.wikitude.com/tour/wikitude-world-browser

WORDLENS LITE

Screenshot:

**Figure 3.5.   Word Lens Lite. The mobile interface tool offers text recognition and trans-
lation using the device's built-in camera.**

What it does: The WordLens Lite app translates text from the surrounding environment to another language. The screenshot above is illustrating how a pedestrian exploring a new area can get sign text translated on the fly using a phone running a WordLens app. This app is the free version of WordLens; the full software download has additional language packs.

Use case: The uses inside of libraries for translation tools such as this may be more effective than the outdoors and pedestrian needs. The reason for this is that the user in the library is looking at a test that is most likely printed in a straight line, in good lighting, and in type that is easy to read. Outside of the library, the use of the app is complicated by the fact that the lighting may be poor, the camera might be angled, and the signage will not be designed to be scanned by an optical character recognition tool; the indoor library uses will actually be more compelling and, one might hypothesize, the textual content of scanned books will work better for the app. This tool could replace the reference collection content of foreign dictionaries. Additionally, if your library has a large population of foreign language learners, or those who are learning English as a second language, the language packs that they could download with this tool may be helpful to get started with language comprehension.

Additional use case: Literacy is an important mission for libraries. There are adult populations even of the United States that are functionally illiterate. Tutors in library settings helping with functional literacy skills may wish to use this app as pedagogical support helps to support language learning in the library. What may be possible with this app is the connection of users to language in a way that can offer independence in learning and self-directed learning, too.

What you should know/more information about how it works: Using text recognition software, the camera grabs an image from the world and then scans the text. The textual recognition is not always perfect and does require well-lit areas as well as large enough and clean enough text to function properly. While there is pretty good coverage, innovations will be forthcoming and better functionality will come out of the software.

Apps like this to look out for in the future: In the future we can expect to see more efficient recognition of words by apps like this, and possibly as other software companies enter this sphere we will see a greater connection among textual recognition and other library tools, such as dictionaries, and reference sources like encyclopedias and even Wikipedia. Perhaps the additional language dictionaries will come down in price, or be free, after more companies are able to offer comparable services.

Consulted: https://play.google.com/store/apps/details?id=com.quest visual.wordlens

Chapter 4

Productivity Apps
for Library Services

This type of app will look like a mobile browser window. Its use is task-oriented. Users will be able to specify certain information to receive based on an immediate library need. As an example of a productivity app utilized in a library setting, consider the user who would like to be notified when an item is returned. This "book notification" app can help to give your users up-to-the-minute information about items when the status changes.

ABC NEWS

Screenshot:

Figure 4.1.   ABC News. Visual headlines and surfacing top stories are a feature of news apps.

What it does: The app is organized by five tabs: top news, a module for
shows, a local ABC News section, any user-created saved searches, and a
video module. In the top news section, the user can switch the feed from
technology, travel, money, politics, investigative, health, entertainment,
international, and U.S. The ABC News mobile app is set up for the user to
decide how to receive the type of ABC News that they want to get.

Use case: This app is a great referral source for public services staff that is helping users stay up-to-date on current news. For credible up-to-date information and breaking news, sources like the ABC News app can push out the news that users want current updates on. Consider a user of the library that doesn't have access to traditional desktop and Internet access; perhaps she is in the library just to get current news from the public computing access the library provides. If such a patron had access to a smartphone with a data plan, she could download the ABC News app and continue her browsing and information search away from the library—it would be particularly useful for getting push notifications of news items, but would also provide the added convenience of not having to physically visit the library in order to get online access to news sources.

Additional use case: As an additional use case consider a librarian in a public library setting delivering a workshop on mobile applications. For certain populations of the library, being able to understand new mobile apps may prove a conceptual leap. This is understandable since mobile applications sometimes do not have desktop-based analogs. For a library workshop that features a known quantity like the ABC News platform, the leader of the workshop has an easier job explaining and introducing the functionalities of mobile computing possibilities—the video feeds, up-to-date notifications, and push capabilities. Users may be more likely to try out mobile applications if they can get introduced to a mobile app that they understand the conceptual underpinnings of.

What you should know/more information about how it works: There is a select list of local news providers that are currently feeding in news stories to the ABC app—but not every news area/location is going to have a local feed. On first load of the ABC app, it does ask to use your location and requests push notification settings for the application.

Apps like this to look out for in the future: News organizations are certainly trying to redefine and rework their traditional offerings for a mobile world. Since mobile first initiatives are likely to grow over time, users should expect that more news stations will be moving to provide their content from the handheld devices that users carry. In the future news organizations may provide premium mobile content as they seek to reach out to an important and growing segment of information platforms.

Consulted: https://itunes.apple.com/us/app/abc-news/id300255638?mt=8

AMAZON.COM MOBILE

Screenshot:

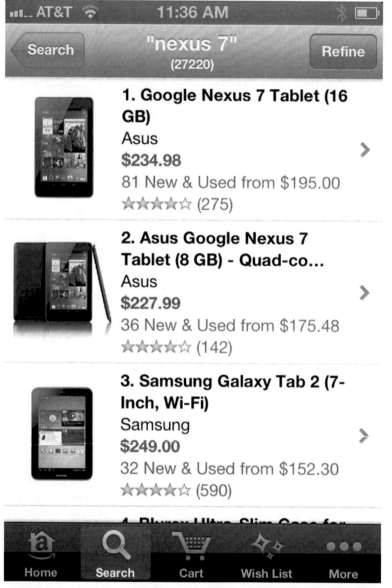

Figure 4.2.   Amazon.com Mobile. The mobile view of Amazon includes many of the features that users have come to expect from the full web store available on a desktop browser.

What it does: This app supports the usual Amazon-type experience of searching and buying books, in an easy-to-use mobile-friendly display. You can access previously saved items from your cart, and also access items from your wishlist. Included in the mobile app is the function to log in using your previously set up Amazon credentials. The mobile component, which takes advantage of your phone's camera as a barcode scanner, will allow you to get price comparisons from the Amazon website, and you can also use your camera for image recognition of products on the website.

Use case: The value of something like Amazon Mobile rests in the data that users generate on the site. Of particular importance is the ability to get recommendations for books based on a single item of interest. Using these suggestions in the context of library book stacks browsing makes for a compelling user experience, where users can connect to additional resources based on location and interest.

Additional use case: Consider users in a bookstore who are contemplating what to buy next. They can compare, with this app, the bookstore prices against what is available for purchase on Amazon.com. Since inputting long strings of text is not easy on mobile devices, the scanning and image input of the phone (searching by media) is an important consideration for mobile, contextual needs of users.

What you should know/more information about how it works: The app functions similarly to the online bookselling site. The mobile version seems to have included user preferences based on how first-time users browse mobile websites, with expanded mobile list elements and helpful drop-down menus of additional, consumer-driven content.

Apps like this to look out for in the future: Amazon isn't just a print bookselling company; it is looking to be the content provider of electronic books. Future apps it builds will be in an attempt to solidify its position as the e-book content provider of the mobile web.

Consulted: http://itunes.apple.com/us/app/amazon-mobile/id297606951?mt=8

AMERICAN AIRLINES

Screenshot:

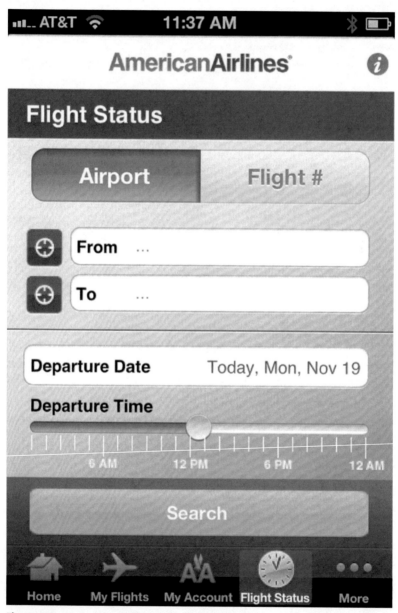

Figure 4.3. American Airlines. The flight status information modules is one of the highlights of the mobile American Airlines app.

What it does: The American Airlines mobile app offers much of the functionality that is available on the standard website, and then also some helpful mobile-only additions. One of the more compelling uses for the American Airlines app at the airport is to access your "mobile boarding pass." The mobile boarding pass could be scanned in at your gate in order to board the plane without needing a paper pass—simply scan the barcode that comes through your app interface to board the plane. Another helpful in-the-airport feature of the mobile app is the ability to view maps of the airport and then also see flight status and gate updates from the mobile app as well.

Use case: An app like this for library services is most likely going to reach your patron base that is composed of travelers or those getting ready to take a vacation. When the summer vacation season rolls around in your library and you are making travel guide websites, or book displays, the library will want to also consider making a list of selected mobile apps that help travelers in the airport and on the go. While American Airlines is not the only air travel company to offer a mobile app, some of the key features you would want to see are available through this interface.

What you should know/more information about how it works: In order to get your flight information, standby list updates, and current seating assignments you need to actually log in. Login windows inside of a small screen, accessed on-the-go, can be serious barriers to mobile apps, but in the case of a travel app with the type of information that is available here, actually logging in to your account is something that most travelers are willing to be burdened by.

Apps like this to look out for in the future: Travel is one field that mobile computing can help address since it should be made more painless and mobile applications that make travel easier are going to be innovating into the future.

Consulted: https://itunes.apple.com/us/app/american-airlines/id382698565?mt=8

BBC NEWS

Screenshot:

Figure 4.4. BBC News. The tile organization of news stories by category makes the breadth of coverage easy to navigate from a small screen device.

What it does: This is the mobile application for the BBC website. It includes a live radio stream, and a well-organized and easy-to-understand layout of top news items which has a very nice visual appeal. The news stories are formatted here for browsing on mobile display and include a helpful way to bump up the text if the reader requires the text to be larger (not typically considered for any kind of new reading environment). Also, options to share news stories are available from the article-level page.

Use case: This app can be useful in a library setting as an addition to the library's tablets or other mobile browsing devices. The content is free to read and easy to navigate. There are numerous considerations for users here, including the ability to forward and post articles to social networking feeds.

Additional use case: Another use case for the library would be to make use of in-app functionality whereby librarians making use of any kind of staff-facing mobile device would be able to forward the news items from their Twitter feeds or library Facebook feeds. This would be a way to reach out to a patron base and keep it informed of recent news events that may be relevant or important to the surrounding community.

What you should know/more information about how it works: A very nice reformatting job here from the original BBC website. The visual layout makes sense and recent articles are organized by their associated images. The app makes use of a horizontal and vertical panning approach to browsing, which makes news feeds easy to browse, and allows the app designers and users to pan over more content while still being able to navigate the mobile interface. BBC News app does a nice job of making its app full of information while not overwhelming the user with display elements.

Apps like this to look out for in the future: The radio feed is an interesting addition to the mobile world, as one would have expected perhaps video feeds to be delivered, especially with the content that the BBC can offer and deliver to users. Perhaps in later versions of the BBC app we can expect to see video and rich multimedia content that is available through live streaming and the web.

Consulted: http://itunes.apple.com/gb/app/bbc-news/id377382255?mt=8

BIBLE

Screenshot:

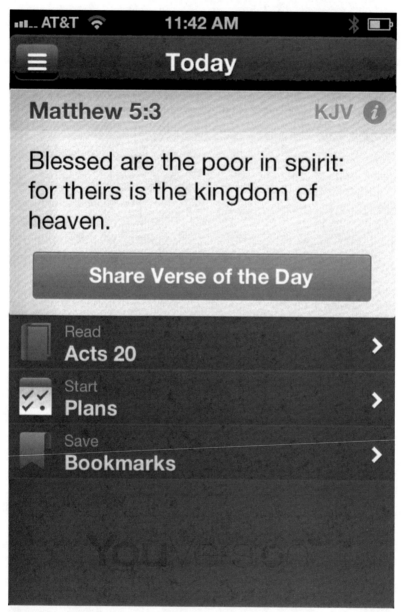

Figure 4.5. Bible. One of the Bible mobile app features includes a verse of the day option.

What it does: The Bible is a popular reference source around the world. This app provides the reader with translations of the text of the Bible in some thirty languages. In addition there are ample social networking integration tools—so you could theoretically post passages that are of interest to you to your Facebook or Twitter accounts.

Use case: Your library users may want to access the text of the Bible for reference while on the go. If your library community is one in which this resource is popular and you cannot provide enough print copies for the user base, it may make sense to point to online and mobile app sources of the Bible as well. The mobile app has a pretty useful search tool, so users who are trying to remember verses while away from their computer may find this a useful resource.

What you should know/more information about how it works: The app requests push notification approval on first load—you can disable here or later in settings if you don't want to receive notifications. With your free download of the app you get a free login, but also, you have to log in on first load; one helpful way to avoid having to remember yet another password would be to log in with your Facebook account or Google Plus account.

Apps like this to look out for in the future: It is interesting to see that software companies are using such popular resources as the Bible as a means to build platforms. This app is one example of a way that Internet businesses are repackaging these popular resources into social platforms and engagement tools. In the future more high-demand resources may see similar re-use and repackaging.

Consulted: https://itunes.apple.com/us/app/bible/id282935706?mt=8

BING

Screenshot:

Figure 4.6.   Bing. The mobile view of the Bing search allows for easy-to-understand filtered searching.

What it does: The Bing app is the mobile interface for the search engine from Microsoft. The engine includes data integration with Facebook "likes" and the use of phone-specific searching. The aspects of the mobile application that incorporate phone-specific searching include making use of a Bing component called Bing Vision for QR codes and other barcodes. This could be very interesting for library engagement in the stacks. The mobile app supports search voice, which allows you to make use of the speech-to-Internet search.

Use case: Within the library stacks a user may have evolving information needs, so the library use case here includes connecting search engine data from Bing with library barcode data. Librarians may try to position library research databases as something distinct from search engines like Bing, however, the case in the library could be made for search engines that work hand in hand with the information search needs within library settings.

What you should know/more information about how it works: There is a lot of the Bing feature set that is familiar to those who use the desktop-based Bing search. What is very interesting here is the ability to use the Flight-Cast feature on the app, a tool that allows users to understand how flight costs are trending and whether or not they should buy their ticket now, or wait until the price will come down.

Apps like this to look out for in the future: Search engine integration into the mobile realm will be a novel area to watch; while many of the giants in this area are looking to understand how to create revenue, the mobile users of search engines are currently enjoying a rather ad-free experience. Something to watch over time is how the advertisements and mobile commerce choices that search giants make will impact the search experience.

Consulted: http://itunes.apple.com/us/app/bing/id345323231?mt-8

CRAIGSLIST MOBILE

Screenshot:

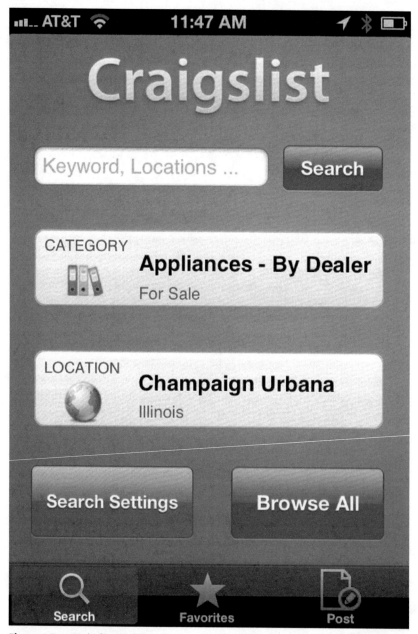

Figure 4.7.   Craigslist Mobile. The category and location filters are helpful search settings on the mobile interface.

What it does: This is the mobile-accessible view of Craigslist. For those unfamiliar with the Craigslist website, it is a helpful resource for buying and selling items locally, renting, and finding apartments or roommates. This app allows you to post available property or items, and also lets you search with helpful filters for items you may be interested in purchasing. The three main tabs of the app include a search module, a favorites module, and a post section.

Use case: Library users, especially in public library settings, will look for community-based deals and low-cost options for furniture or for renting. While public library support can help start users on searching for these items, it makes sense also to recommend these tools for users outside of library settings. By recommending to library patrons the mobile version of a page like Craigslist, there is the potential for ongoing search assistance. One particularly helpful feature for the Craigslist Mobile site is the inclusion of advanced searching functionality. A user is able to filter by price and item in the search module of the app.

Additional use case: There is also a "jobs" category here that could be useful to the library patron that is currently seeking employment. While public libraries have certainly been offering services to help out-of-work individuals identify key resources that would help them apply for work, this app could be a way to continue to support the job search process from the convenience of a library patron's mobile phone.

What you should know/more information about how it works: The Craigslist Mobile site will look as familiar to you as the desktop version, but especially streamlined for the mobile app. In some ways this makes it easier to find what you are looking for while searching, since the functionality of the rather spare text site is paired down to just a few simple search elements. One helpful mobile device integration tool is the ability to post photos taken on the phone directly to the Craigslist site. The location-based GPS detection will automatically do location filtering based on your current location.

Apps like this to look out for in the future: Popular websites that get reformatted for mobile are a current trend of the mobile environment. However, one paradigm shift over the next year to watch will be mobile-first initiatives, and a growing number of mobile-only services—these include services that are only mobile applications and make use of location, networked connectivity, and other "on-site" uses. The transition to mobile-only services is a coming wave in mobile application design, especially as more people access information solely from their handheld devices.

Consulted: https://itunes.apple.com/us/app/craigslist-mobile-for-iphone/id430667358?mt=8

DICTIONARY.COM

Screenshot:

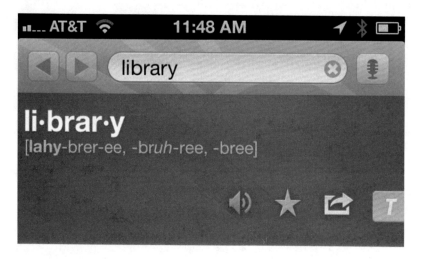

- *noun, pl.* **-brar·ies.**

1. a place set apart to contain books, periodicals, and other material for reading, viewing, listening, study, or reference, as a room, set of rooms, or building where books may be read or borrowed.

2. a public body organizing and maintaining such an establishment.

3. a collection of manuscripts, publications,

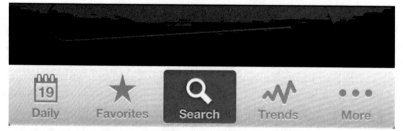

Figure 4.8.   Dictionary.com. A helpful feature of the dictionary mobile app is the listing of multiple or alternative definitions.

What it does: This app is organized by the following tabs: the word of the day, a favorites section, a dictionary search, and a trends module. The trends part of the app shows words that are recently popular searches of the dictionary by other users; with the location-sharing service enabled in the app you are able to see what the trending search words are in your geographic area. The search module allows you to search for a definition in the dictionary, or you can search for similar words in the thesaurus tab.

Use case: Library users may want to engage with both the dictionary's content and that of a thesaurus. The app will also automatically send you a word of the day, which may be useful for library users who are either not native speakers or are looking to increase their vocabulary.

What you should know/more information about how it works: Like many of the new tools written about here, this app also requests permission to send you push notifications. The app, on first load, also asks about using your current location.

Apps like this to look out for in the future: This is a traditional-type reference source that was already made a bit obsolete by the availability of text autocomplete and spelling correction in its search interface; however, it has new usefulness by packaging word-of-the-day features into the software, as well as providing both definitions and thesaurus entries for words.

Consulted: https://itunes.apple.com/us/app/dictionary.com-dictionary/id308750436?mt=8

EPICURIOUS

Screenshot:

Figure 4.9. Epicurious. The home view of the app is organized by meal types and includes useful seasonal suggestions.

What it does: This is a recipe app. You can also make use of this app as a shopping list service, too. From the home screen of Epicurious the user can search through recipes for breakfast, lunch, and dinner. On the home screen is an easy meals recipe finder. From the search function of the app a user can input a desired ingredient or ingredients from which to build a meal and will get a list of suggestions to search through. There is a favorites tab here as well that allows you to save recipes.

Use case: Useful on the go, is the ability to search for ingredients that you have and then see what recipes you can make from them. You can use the information to then complete your meal for the evening.

Additional use case: This app would be a useful tool to introduce non-technology types into the world of mobile applications. Users who may not think of apps as particularly useful or time-saving may actually find this tool a significant time-saver and immediately useful for day-to-day type of activities.

What you should know/more information about how it works: The app is pulling data from the popular website http://www.epicurious.com/. The great reformatting to mobile has preserved an important part of this website which includes the reviews of recipes generated and contributed by users of the site. This can give users a helpful insight as to what they are actually getting into when they attempt a new recipe.

Apps like this to look out for in the future: This app is certainly one of the more practical apps for people to make use of for their daily eating needs.

Consulted: http://www.epicurious.com/; http://itunes.apple.com/app/epicurious-recipes-shopping/id312101965?mt=8

EVERNOTE

Screenshot:

Figure 4.10.   Evernote. A useful organizational tool for the items in Evernote are the Notebook views which collect and compile the notes you make.

What it does: One of the most popular productivity apps on the iTunes App Store, Evernote will provide one-stop mobile access to all your notes, organized based on tags that you create. The library user simply needs to log in and create an account. Once you do that you can save content here and share among different devices. With a nod to the collaborative learning taking place in most higher education institutions, users will have the option of sharing their notebooks with other Evernote accounts. Your Evernote "notebooks" (collections of notes that you create) are available from any device that can access Evernote.

Use case: For library users involved in book clubs or literacy programs, actually keeping track of what you read and when you read it can get to be a hassle. There are a number of places in the cloud you could store this information. And, like many cloud-based uses reviewed for mobile apps, everything is stored off your phone. If you think that users will remember books by their covers more easily than their titles, have the user take a picture of the book that they are reading and save that image to an Evernote notebook. That way, when they need readers' advisory information, all they need to do is consult the images from their previous books. The power of the Evernote app is the integration of camera components and software.

Additional use case: Installing the Evernote client on your desktop system could help to support the information needs of your library patrons on the go as well. What Evernote excels at is an interface for desktop access that is very simple to understand and also easy to use. The desktop view of the Evernote app allows you to access the mobile Evernote information.

What you should know/more information about how it works: The Evernote mobile and desktop combo is successful for developing an easy-to-search and easy-to-understand interface. Other companies won't easily replicate the quick search and self-organizing tagging features. Additional components that weren't covered in the use case above include creating a voice memo with your phone and then storing this into your account.

Apps like this to look out for in the future: An optimistic view of what would be great to see in future apps like this would be consideration for the limitations of mobile and supplement them with the advantages of desktop; stable access to the web, larger screen, and then also the keyboard.

Consulted: http://evernote.com/

FACETIME

Screenshot:

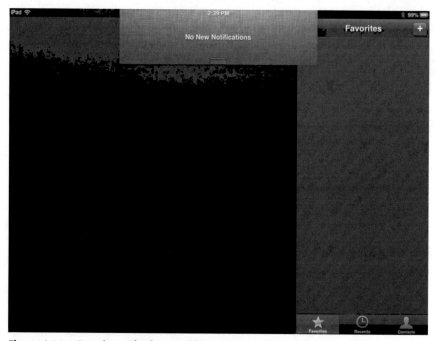

Figure 4.11.   Facetime. The lower right corner of the Facetime app allows users to organize their calls and contacts. The main view in the middle is where your caller on the other end of the video chat will appear.

What it does: The Facetime app comes standard on the iPhone and the iPad versions (2 and 3) that include front-facing cameras. The app usually uses the WiFi of the phone in order to achieve a kind of video chat by way of mobile phone to another device that also has the Facetime app running—this can be another Apple computer like the MacBook Pro or the iMac (which also have front-facing cameras). Some data plan providers may allow you to make Facetime calls but it may not be guaranteed for all data plans.

Use case: Since this is an app that comes already loaded with your shiny new product, you might be wondering why I am including it here on a book on mobile apps. The connection among various service points in larger libraries with embedded librarians may make this app useful as a way to connect to various experts in a library system, who may be able to help with research and consultations without being physically present.

Consider also that reaching individuals in front of their computers by video chat may be easier than reaching them by email, especially if you haven't charged your cell phone, or calling is not an option, but Internet access is available.

What you should know/more information about how it works: You'll need to do some set up of your Facetime on a laptop before you can get going with this. So if you want to have Facetime as an option, go ahead and do a practice run with your hardware first. Find some collaborators in your library and video chat for fun. Also when you absolutely need Facetime to be working, it is best (as with pretty much any technology tool) to try a dry run of the app with a colleague first. That way when you need it to be functioning you will have already tried out the possibilities of the app and understood any bandwidth limitations or video possibilities, too.

Apps like this to look out for in the future: Given the bandwidth that these video chat apps make use of, we can't expect much innovation in the app domain until the infrastructure costs of provider data plans adapt. We can, however, expect the ultra-high-speed Internet coming with fiber to help make smart objects possible in residences, but don't expect your phone to be immediately part of that innovation.

Consulted: http://www.apple.com/iphone/built-in-apps/facetime.html

FIREFOX (ANDROID)

Screenshot:

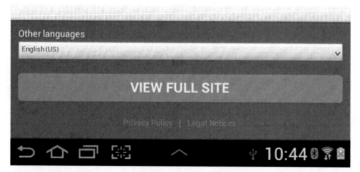

Figure 4.12. Firefox for Android. The app supports installation of browser plugins just like the desktop version.

What it does: It is the mobile version of the popular Firefox web browser. As a free app it can supplement the native browser that comes loaded on any Android device. You can download this to an Android phone or Android tablet and replicate the browsing experience you are accustomed to, like a tabbed browsing experience and quick web browsing from a mobile app interface.

Use Case: For those making use of many of the popular Android tablet devices, having an alternative browser may be preferable to the standard vendor specific browsers that come loaded with the device. There are a number of parallels with the desktop Firefox browser that new mobile users may find helpful—these include accessing multiple tabs in the browsing window along with the option to search and install plugins that are made for the Firefox for Android app.

Additional Use Case: Libraries with software development staff may have browser plugins that they currently are offering their patron base for enhanced access to resources. One alternative use case that developers may want to make use of is to set up their existing plugins for the Firefox for Android mobile app.

What you should know/more information about how it works: Those who are new to mobile apps or new to tablet devices would find this app a welcome addition to their browser options since there aren't a lot of new mobile interaction or mobile specific conventions utilized in the app. The browser has helpful privacy control features like the "Do Not Track" setting where your browser can indicate to websites that you do not want your browsing behavior to be logged. Note though that currently stored information, like log in credentials stored in the Firefox browser will then get cleared out.

Apps like this to look out for in the future: Mozilla is embracing open web standards and vendor independent tools. Look for apps that come from the Mozilla foundation as articulating this open web standards conceptualization. It is likely that their future development road map will choose web apps using HTML5 and CSS and JavaScript over native development environments that use compiled languages like Objective C or closed development environments.

Consulted: https://play.google.com/store/apps/details?id=org.mozilla .firefox; http://support.mozilla.org/en-US/kb/how-do-i-turn-do-not -track-feature-mobile

FLIPBOARD

Screenshot:

Figure 4.13.   Flipboard. Compelling visual navigation of news stories is the primary appeal for this app.

What it does: The Flipboard app is a visual newsreader tool. The app features integration with news feeds from online news sources like BBC World, The Atlantic, Al Jazeera, and many more. Social feeds can be incorporated here as well, since you are able to pull in your Twitter feeds, Facebook news feed, and Google Plus posts and see those feeds side by side with trending news topics. The Flipboard app also offers a compelling user experience in that it is visually well designed (making heavy, prominent use of graphics) and makes for an easy-to-understand, visually compelling news-reading experience.

Use case: The public library setting may be best suited for leisurely browsing of popular news resources. With the onset of tablet-based news reading, public libraries may want to rethink and reconceptualize what it means to provide access to current periodicals. Consider users in a tablet browsing space of your library. The library could set up kiosk locations where preloaded news items—titles that the library currently subscribes to—could be featured in the Flipboard application.

Additional use case: A librarian could also use the Flipboard application to stay current in specific subject areas. A passing interest in most subjects will serve any public librarian well in answering reference desk questions, particularly any science or technology topics. If you find your knowledge needs updating in technology or science areas, you could make use of the Flipboard application while at a research desk for subject-specific news items like current science topics or current technology topics.

What you should know/more information about how it works: There is also convenient integration with Google's Reader software so that you could make use of the app to display a news-magazine-like app for your blog feeds. You can also create a login to map to your Facebook credentials and other social networks.

Apps like this to look out for in the future: Visual innovation in mobile app design is beginning to be a bit more mainstreamed. Future news-viewing apps will likely grow in popularity, and at the same time these apps are likely to be specifically used on tablets, especially since the larger screen size will be best suited for the visual design choices of the app developers.

Consulted: https://itunes.apple.com/us/app/flipboard-your-social-news/id358801284?mt=8

FOX NEWS

Screenshot:

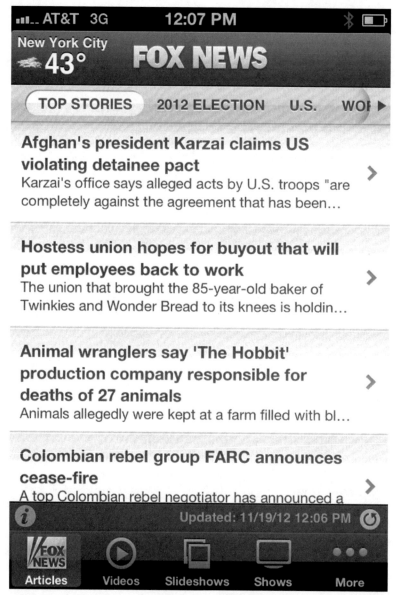

Figure 4.14. Fox News. The popular stories surfacing near the top of the navigation makes it easy to locate relevant and up-to-date news information through your mobile device.

What it does: This is a news app. It is a true multimedia experience. From the Fox News app you can stream the contents of Fox News shows and tab to slideshows and other videos, as well as read the text content of Fox News articles. From the app you can also add favorite articles that will be stored for your viewing later. There is a weather function in the "more" tab as well as access to the stream of FOX News Radio.

Use case: Users that are so inclined, in a library setting, may want to access the live news feeds but not have the full media available—they can turn the device horizontally and receive an experience not unlike the traditional TV-viewing experience, with news ticker, feature stories, and the like.

What you should know/more information about how it works: This app asks to send you push notification. You can configure these push notifications in your settings, or choose not to receive any notifications.

Apps like this to look out for in the future: The future of news apps is indicated here by the increasing use of both video content and radio content, combined in the mobile experience.

Consulted: https://itunes.apple.com/us/app/fox-news/id367623543?mt=8

Chapter 4

GASBUDDY

Screenshot:

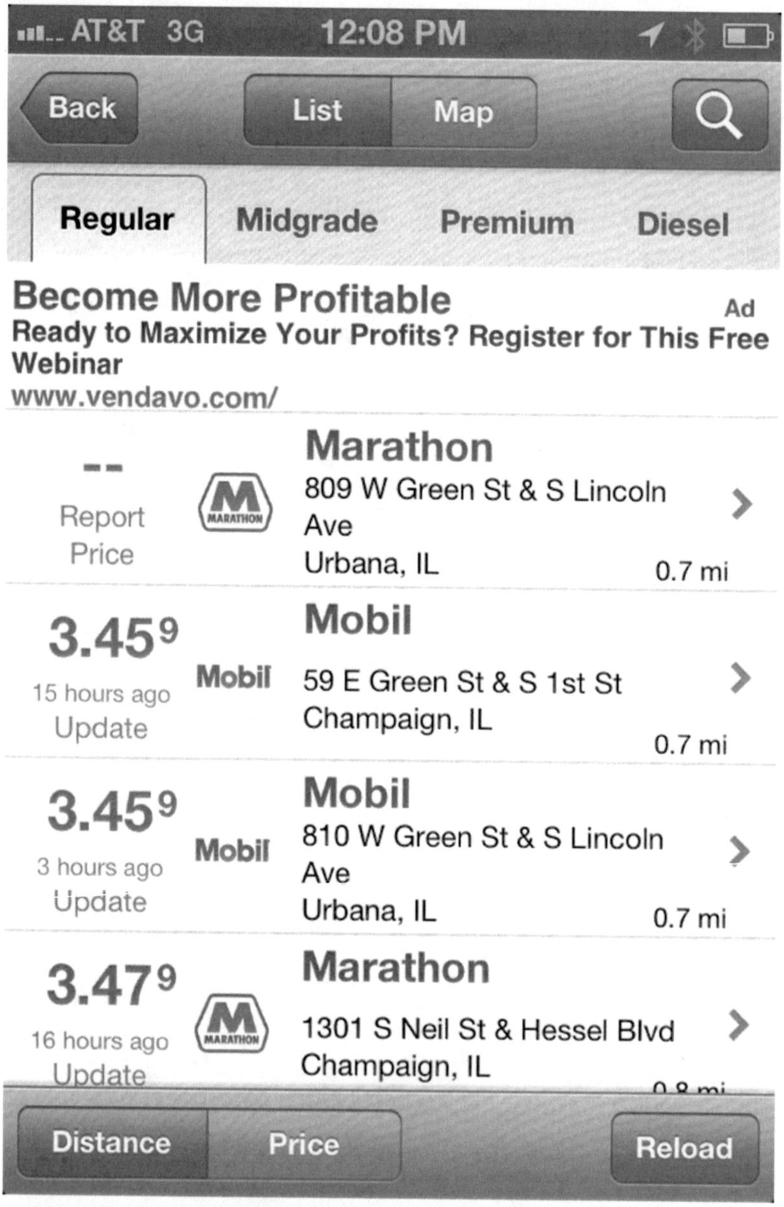

Figure 4.15.   Gas Buddy. The nearest gas locations can come in handy if you are driving in a new area and looking for low-cost gas options.

What it does: This is an app that uses your location to identify the nearest gas stations. You can also use the apps filters to display the lowest-cost gas nearest to your location. The app functionality offers three modules: you can log in, share a price, or configure the app settings. Since this is a free app, it does feature mobile advertising from the main and secondary menus, which can be a bit distracting, particularly in the case of mobile browsing.

Use case: For library patrons that are living and working in areas where driving is a necessity or public transportation is not an option, an app like GasBuddy can be a cost-saver, particularly as prices for gasoline continue to rise. You can search by city or by zip code, so you don't have to necessarily search by your detected location—this may be useful for users who are commuting or interested in buying gas in another, perhaps less costly, nearby area.

What you should know/more information about how it works: There are some built-in benefits for making use of this app, not just locating low-cost gas stations. There is a rewards system that you can get plugged into by joining and then logging into the site with your membership. Basically, you get points for reporting gasoline prices to the app, and then you also get the opportunity to win a drawing for $250 every week.

Apps like this to look out for in the future: The interesting social component to this app is the collaborative way that users seed the app with gas prices. They help to keep the app content current, and by doing so, they keep the app valuable to others. This is a fairly compelling example of crowd-sourced public-benefit-type applications in a private-public partnership.

Consulted: https://itunes.apple.com/us/app/gasbuddy-find-cheap-gas -prices/id406719683?mt=8

Chapter 4

GOODREADS

Screenshot:

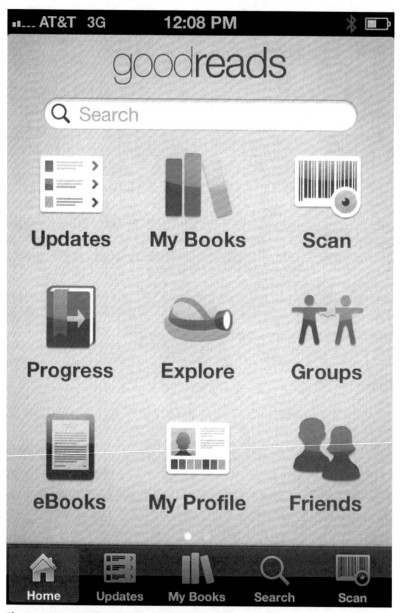

Figure 4.16. Goodreads. The icon layout of the main home screen provides an easy to understand overview of the total app functionality.

What it does: The Goodreads mobile app supports some of the common desktop uses of Goodreads. These include searching for a book (either in your library Goodreads collection, or the Goodreads database of books) and looking at your friends' updates (the progress they are making on books, or the comments and reviews they are making on the books they are reading). However, the mobile version also allows for some additional uses, which include scanning a book's barcode. This is, of course, of use in libraries, as it would be in any commerce-type location.

Use case: This is definitely the app for book lovers. Those who love to read can access their reading lists and create and edit these reading lists while on their phone, in libraries, or of course in bookstores. Oftentimes, as the case may be, the desire to remember to read a book is not recorded—this is something that the Goodreads app can help to address, so you don't have to remember what is next on your reading list. You can also use the app to take a quick glance at what your friends are reading and what they think about what their friends are reading—a highly social utility for those who enjoy books and discussing them.

Additional use case: Besides learning what your friends like and enjoy reading, you can also edit and create your own reviews of books, or even just catalog your favorites. It is a nice feature to go through and rank which books you would want to read again, and this may help to generate future recommendations of other books to read.

What you should know/more information about how it works: As with most social-type apps, this one features the common "set up a profile and then find people you know" type of interface. It also includes optional integration with your Facebook and Twitter accounts—so that you could post updates to books you are reading or reviews of books to your news feeds or updates inside of those social platforms.

Apps like this to look out for in the future: This app is actually a very good model for the ways that library mobile apps (by this I mean library-developed apps) should be developed—it has personalization features, it uses elements of the standard phone (like the barcode scanner), and it connects your data with other social networking platforms.

Consulted: http://itunes.apple.com/us/app/goodreads/id355833469?mt=8

Chapter 4

GOOGLE DRIVE

Screenshot:

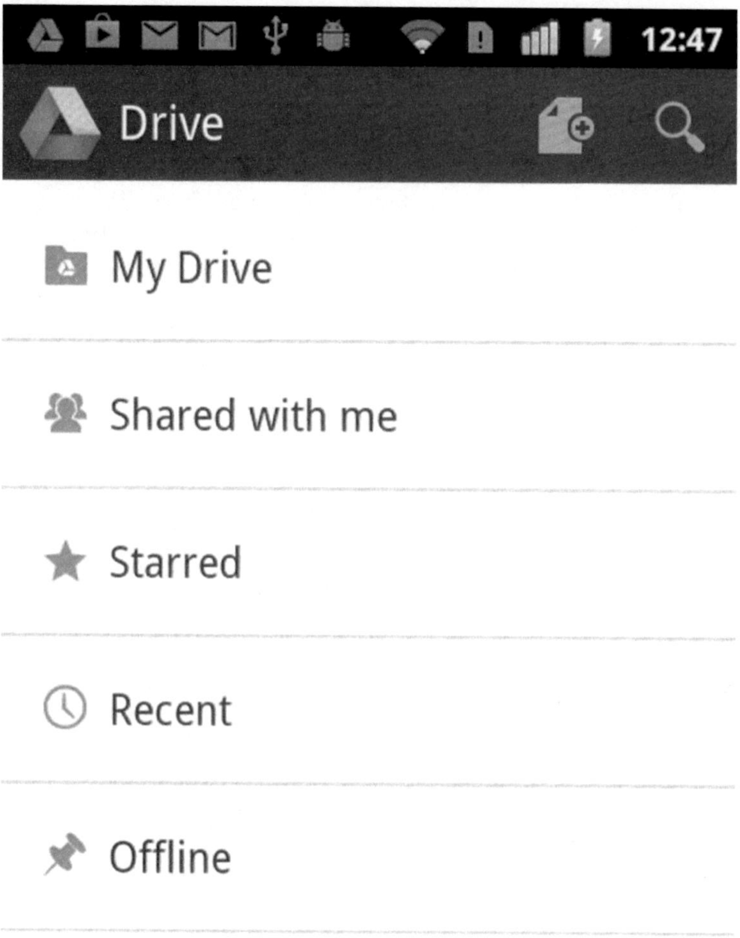

Figure 4.17.   Google Drive. The simple and easy to navigate interface allows the user to access files stored in their Google Drive account.

What it does: This is the mobile interface to the popular Google Drive web-based tool, that place where you not only store, but also edit spreadsheets, presentations, and text files in the cloud. If you aren't familiar with the Google Drive experience, this is due to the relative newness of the tool. Google Drive is a reboot of the Google Docs experience. With Google Drive you can have a "drop-box" like folder on your desktop and sync anything that is online in your Google Drive to your desktop-based system or mobile system. The marketing for this new service is that Google intends to connect you with your files no matter where you are and what device you are using.

There are some benefits to being on your phone and accessing Google Drive. Since you are also on your phone, it allows you to take image captures of documents and then store them in the cloud. Also, given the integration with your phone, you are able to quickly share information with the contact list in your phone as well. Similar to the Dropbox application, you are able to download documents to access in an offline mode.

Use case: Within the library domain there is one resource that our patrons cannot get enough of—computing. Some may argue for books, but more contemporary is the need for computing resources in the library. Theoretically, the Google Drive app could be loaded onto a tablet computer which the library could make available for library usage. This would help to supplement the computing resources, and at the same time leverage the resources that Google makes available freely.

Additional use case: Librarians might want to recommend this tool for users who need to scan text documents on the go—Google has a nice feature built in which allows you to take a picture of the document and which uses Google's own character-recognition software to convert the image to text.

What you should know/more information about how it works: This app is part of Google's offering of cloud-based productivity services. The functionality of this app is increased by the user's familiarity with and previous use of Google's online services.

Apps like this to look out for in the future: If past practice is any indication, Google pretty much innovates continuously, which shouldn't surprise any reader of this book. The surprising thing about cloud-based computing is the proliferation of cloud services into mobile, and this bodes well for devices, since at a certain point the devices do not have the same hardware and hard drive capability of desktop-based systems. What we'll see in the future is the cloud helping to power your productivity experience. The things that device makers need to catch up on are the screen size and keyboard affordances. At the moment these are holding true productivity on the mobile devices back.

Consulted: https://play.google.com/store/apps/details?id=com.google.android.apps.docs

GOOGLE EARTH

Screenshot:

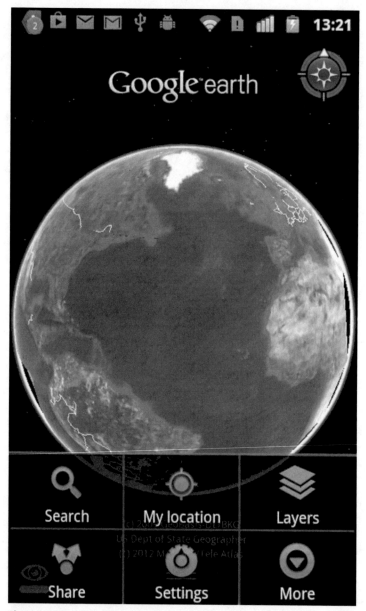

Figure 4.18. Google Earth. The touch screen of any mobile device makes it easy to explore Google Earth information.

What it does: This is the mobile version of Google Earth. The iOS version allows for multi-touch manipulation and layering of views on the mobile interface. Of course, another additional value of Google Earth on a mobile device is the ability to use your device's current location for a fly-over view display. From this fly-over display you can see geo-referenced information relevant to your location. The linked information usually includes a landmark or image relevant to your location. 3-D image exploration is also included, as well as a search by voice within the Google Earth app.

Use case: Librarians can make use of Google Earth as a way to add information to their community geography. To add your community snapshots into Google Earth, you could create a kind of exploration game—not necessarily a treasure hunt, but something akin to a tour. If your library had archived collections of the community, you could associate these image data with locations on Google Earth coordinates.

Additional use case: In major metropolitan areas the app is most likely more useful since these are places where the building typography lends itself to the panoramic views.

What you should know/more information about how it works: Again, becoming familiar with the desktop version of this service will help to underscore some of the more breathtaking things you can do with Google Earth.

Apps like this to look out for in the future: At least one major competitor is getting into the geographic visualization and panorama sphere. This means that some innovation will be occurring, especially in the mobile sphere, for visualizing overhead and street-level graphics, including three-dimensional overlays.

Consulted: http://news.cnet.com/8301-1023_3-57480273-93/googles-neato-3d-city-view-arrives-on-ios-today/; http://itunes.apple.com/us/app/google-earth/id293622097?mt=8

GOOGLE PLAY BOOKS

Screenshot:

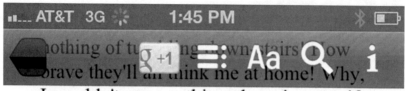

I wouldn't say anything about it, even if
I fell off the top of the house!" (Which
was very likely true.)

Down, down, down. Would the fall
never come to an end? "I wonder how
many miles I've fallen by this time?"
she said aloud. "I must be getting
somewhere near the centre of the earth.
Let me see: that would be four thousand
miles down, I think—" (for, you see,
Alice had learnt several things of this
sort in her lessons in the school-room,
and though this was not a *very* good
opportunity for showing off her
knowledge, as there was no one to listen
to her, still it was good practice to say it

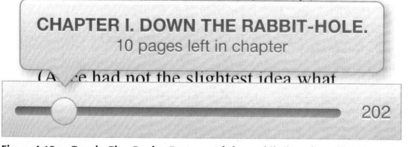

**Figure 4.19. Google Play Books. Features of the mobile interface, like the page
slider shown above, make it easy to navigate books.**

What it does: The Google Play book reader is Google's platform to their online content of e-books, available from Google Play. This may include the scanned content of books that libraries have given to Google that are out of public domain. If the books are in the public domain and Google does not have the copyrights to them, the e-book reader will not be able to provide access to the full text of the book. In addition the books here may also be from publishers who have agreed to have their content hosted by or distributed from the Google Play platform.

Use case: The current version supports over 4 million books, which include *New York Times* bestsellers and a number of freely available books. You can also connect the book you are reading to your Google Plus profile by giving the book you are reading a plus one. This information will then come up on your Google Plus profile linked to the account you have logged in with. This app will be useful for books that are classics, especially if all the copies are frequently checked out from the library. If that is the case, this could be an alternative to ordering many copies of classics, since these are freely available. The only downside is that it isn't quite the same as reading the paper version, since the reader may be viewing the page on the small screen of an iPhone or other smaller mobile device.

Additional use case: The iOS version of this app also offers voice-over support. This feature could be quite useful for those with vision impairment, but also would be a helpful pedagogical tool for those who are just learning to read, for the voice-over support would speak aloud the contents of the page to the user of the app. This may help those for whom English is a second language.

What you should know/more information about how it works: Any of the social integration tools like the Google Plus feature, where you can "+1" a book in the app, require that you have used your Google Plus account to log in. Additionally, the offline reading for the app works if you have previously downloaded the content to your device. This way when you are not connected to WiFi or your phone does not have data coverage, you'll still be able to read from your mobile device.

Apps like this to look out for in the future: Google Play is looking to have a deeper content strategy for media types. The previous instantiation of Google books was the Google App Store, and so as it expands its offerings to items outside of apps it is providing book content, like the content of this app, but it is also looking to deliver additional media content, like music content—Google Play is getting to be similar in design to the iTunes App Store.

Consulted: https://play.google.com/store/apps/details?id=com.google .android.apps.books; http://support.google.com/googleplay/bin/answer .py?hl=en&p=books_androidapp&answer=188708&rd=1

GOOGLE SEARCH MOBILE

Screenshot:

Figure 4.20. Google Search Mobile. The search interface allows next generation search by media queries like voice or image searching.

What it does: The Google Search app on an iOS device can use your location for delivering local search results. Inside of the search, you can use the Goggles feature, which can scan images and text and then send this scanned content into a Google search. The textual recognition inside of Goggles is fairly accurate. This free app can then also translate scanned text from the phone, too.

Included here is a search-by-voice feature that allows you to speak your search query into the phone and perform a Google search this way.

Finally, the Google Search mobile page also includes links to its other mobile apps, including Gmail, Google Plus, Currents, Translate, Voice, Shopper, Earth, Latitude, and Books.

Use case: On the go, the Google Search mobile app can be a real quality-of-life enhancer, since textual and image data can be inputted into the phone, and then Google can perform a search on this. Consider being in a restaurant and appreciating a work of art, but not being able to identify it. The staff at the restaurant are unable to discern where it came from or the title—as far as anyone knows, the painting has been there as a fixture and cannot be identified. This is where Google Goggles come in quite handy, and all you need to do is activate your app, use the picture search to locate a title of the art, and identify the artist.

Additional use case: What some librarians have been making use of in the library is a software API that allows them to plug in a barcode scanner to their mobile apps and scan library books in the stacks. This is what Google provides in its Goggle implementation on iOS devices—the ability to scan a barcode and then do a search on the identified book title. This library use case could be a low-cost way to do fun and engaging library orientation in the book stacks.

What you should know/more information about how it works: There is a popular optical character-recognition tool inside of the Google app. More than this, Google has image-recognition working inside of the app here as well. But it isn't just the fact that these tools recognize items, it is the ability to search the identified items in a Google search bar and get additional information that is particularly useful.

Apps like this to look out for in the future: Google is pioneering research into streetviews and panoramic-type wayfinding inside of buildings, too. Apps like Google's search in the Google Mobile app will be ported into devices like Google Glasses, prototypes that are just becoming available now.

Consulted: http://www.google.com/mobile/search/

Chapter 4

GOOGLE VOICE

Screenshot:

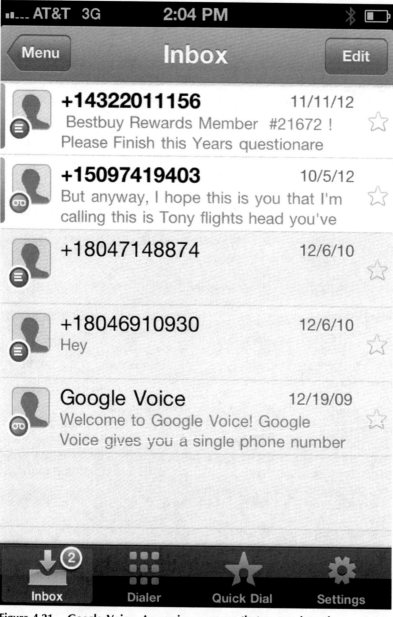

Figure 4.21. Google Voice. Any voice message that comes into the user's account is also converted to text, for easy reading on the go.

What it does: Google Voice is the product from Google that allows you to make cheap international calls as well as answer SMS messages from your desktop. The mobile integration of the Google Voice app will allow you to get transcripts from your voicemails, which is a useful tool for those in need of documentation, or for those who would otherwise have to hand-copy important messages from their mobile phone. Visually panning through voicemail through the Google Voice app is an added benefit to its mobile interface.

Use case: It is fairly common now in public service to answer and interact with users by way of chat reference. To this end, reference services have started to incorporate text (SMS) reference services. With a Google Voice account on a reference desk iPad, librarians that provide reference services would be able to answer any of their patrons' text questions through their previously set up Google Voice account, now available from their roving or office-based iPad.

Additional use case: Visual navigation of voicemails is something that traditional land-line office phones do not support. In library office settings this visual panning through the voicemail can be a useful time saver. For patrons as well, the whole Google Voice infrastructure can amount to cost or time savings, and may replace standard subscription deals such as unlimited texting that are currently purchased with the phone. In order to get this information to your patron base, consider open technology-training workshops around the topic of apps that are free and that can cut down the costs of mobile data plans.

What you should know/more information about how it works: There is a desktop version, of course. You will need to first create a Google Voice account from the Google Voice desktop page here: https://www.google.com/voice. After creating an account you can have all your lines forwarded here, or, alternatively, use it as a backup or text-only (SMS) line.

Apps like this to look out for in the future: The apps of the future that can do what Google Voice is capable of simply represent a new infrastructure around and outside of what classical infrastructures, like traditional SMS, can support. These may include broader access to WiFi infrastructure and hardware that mimics phones, but without their data plans. The low-cost support for international calls is indicative of a mobile market that can provide cost-cutting tools, one that will continue to innovate and reshape the telecommunication marketplace.

Consulted: http://itunes.apple.com/us/app/google-voice/id318698524 ?mt=8

IMDB

Screenshot:

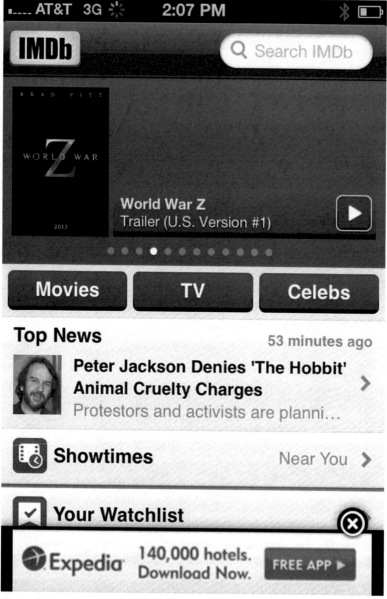

Figure 4.22.   IMDB. Recent, new, and upcoming movie trailers are prominently displayed in the mobile app interface.

What it does: The Internet Movie Database provides reviews, quotes, and cast information, as well as movie trailers for upcoming releases. This is a useful reference resource for when library patrons have movie-specific information needs, especially about contemporary, recently released, or soon-to-be-released movies. The app includes user reviews and organizes popular movies by genre categories.

Use case: If your library offers a media collection that circulates, chances are your users have point-of-need questions about what DVDs to check out next. While every public services worker will be able to answer these questions, a mobile app library IMDb resource can guide users to their next checkout. This app could be affixed to a tablet in the media collection. With a touch screen tablet offering a mobile app search solution, many of your users' point-of-need questions could be answered. An additional "value-add" for this service would be for users to view movie trailers before they actually check out the movie.

What you should know/more information about how it works: On first load the IMDb app asks you if you want to enable location sharing. By enabling location sharing you can get movie show times for the closest theaters.

There is the additional option to create a login here. From the login you could make reviews of movies, ratings, and manage a "watchlist" of movies. You could also log in from your Facebook account, since the app supports Facebook integration for login credentialing.

Apps like this to look out for in the future: Current comments on the iTunes App Store indicate the recent move toward monetizing this service in the mobile realm, so one thing to be on the lookout for with regard to popular apps is the move for developers to try newer, perhaps more intrusive, ways to push ads to users. Another part of this app that is interesting to note in regard to the future is the way that your account can be created from your Facebook login, which is quickly becoming the one login you need on the net in order to credential into other services.

Consulted: https://itunes.apple.com/us/app/imdb-movies-tv/id342792 525?mt=8

ISSRN

Screenshot:

Figure 4.23.   iSSRN. Searching and discovering social science research in the SSRN database through the mobile interface.

What it does: The open online repository of social sciences research, freely searchable by anyone with an Internet connection, now comes to mobile search. Available in the mobile SSRN interface are the same search features users have come to expect from the desktop-based repository. You can do full text searching and view PDFs, where available, on your mobile device. The app allows helpful sharing options by making it easy for you to post article abstracts to your Twitter feed or Facebook timeline or, additionally, share by email.

Use case: Library patrons who may not be able to search the contents of research databases, or licensed research article databases, may want to consider searching the SSRN research data in lieu of subscription access. Perhaps reading on the library patron's mobile phone is cumbersome—in that case emailing PDFs for later viewing or even making use of tablet systems for viewing the PDFs may be the most streamlined way for engaging with this content.

Additional use case: Alternatively, librarians without any access to subscription-based databases may consider making use of openly available archive content such as the data in the SSRN corpus. There are numerous open archives available on the web, and the mobile interface to these archives may make research tasks possible for those without a budget or other access to credible source material.

What you should know/more information about how it works: One probable downside for librarians familiar with database searching is the fact that this service doesn't allow one to perform advanced queries, i.e., it appears that with the single search box users are actually searching the title, author, abstract, and any author-provided keywords for the dataset. This is a problem if the user is after a known item in the set. This is less of a problem if the user is only after a general idea (not comprehensive searching) around a topic and just wants to see what may be out there in the social sciences literature on this topic.

Apps like this to look out for in the future: New federal funding mandates will make it necessary for research output to become available on the open web. As these research reports make their way into the public domain, more requests by way of mobile technologies will be forthcoming—be on the lookout for other open-access repositories making mobile-accessible content.

Consulted: https://itunes.apple.com/us/app/issrn/id334702612?mt=8

KAYAK

Screenshot:

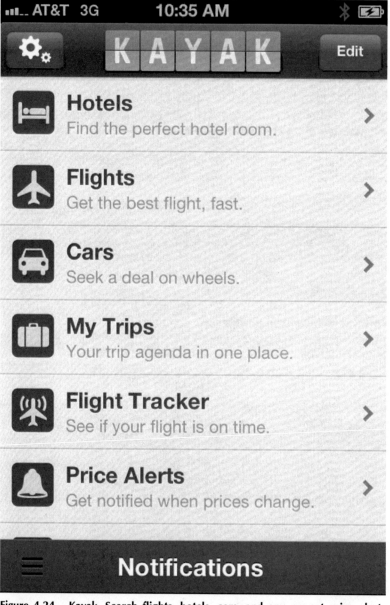

Figure 4.24. Kayak. Search flights, hotels, cars, and any pre-set price alerts from the main Kayak mobile interface.

What it does: The Kayak mobile app allows you to search for and compare flights based on your desired departure dates. By searching multiple airlines and aggregating the results into one easy-to-understand view, it helps you find the lowest prices at the time of search. You can set up alerts for destinations that you are interested in and also book flights for deals that you found on the Kayak site through their mobile app. Hotels and rental cars can also be searched and booked from this app. The power of Kayak is that it checks data across multiple sites and delivers search results showing the lowest-cost options from travel websites.

Use case: For those on-the-go metropolitan types, the easy-to-use one-search paradigm of Kayak will be a valued app. You need to compare prices to get the best deal, right? And in order to compare prices while on the go, you'll be prompted to visit many different websites—lots of different browser windows. Maybe that isn't a big problem for those who are on a desktop system, but on a small form factor mobile device, it will become cumbersome to quickly switch among windows from different travel websites. This is where Kayak is useful. The search interface is a presentation of a kind of federated search across multiple travel sites—airlines, car rental agencies, and also hotel deals.

What you should know/more information about how it works: Kayak is ad-supported, so you aren't paying any money to use its search and booking feature. You don't have to book through Kayak—you can link out to other companies' websites to do the booking yourself. This is an important distinction from popular travel search sites.

Apps like this to look out for in the future: The simple organization and speed of search on the Kayak app is something that more and more mobile applications should be trying to replicate. How and where they do so remains to be seen. Alternatively, an interesting experiment in how federated library systems operate would be to present a Kayak-like interface in which all kinds of searches a user might want to do with library data are presented quickly and efficiently from easy-to-understand search interfaces—mobile and desktop.

Consulted: http://www.kayak.com/about; https://play.google.com/store/apps/details?id=com.kayak.android

KINDLE E-BOOKS READER

Screenshot:

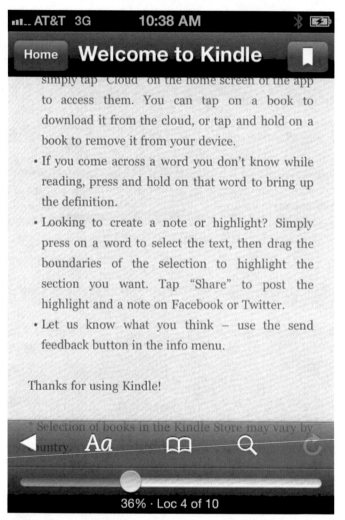

Figure 4.25.   Kindle E-Books Reader. The reader interface includes tools, like the slider bar at the bottom of the screen, for flipping through pages of text.

What it does: This is Amazon's interface for reading Kindle books from your mobile device. Note: it is for viewing Kindle content when you are not reading on your Kindle device. The mobile app on your device is able to sync your last-read page (and highlights, etc.) with something Amazon calls its "Whispersync" technology. There is connection with social networks, so what you can do is highlight words or phrases from this app and then connect/share those words or phrases with your social networks in Facebook, or Twitter, whichever you prefer. If you have previously purchased books, or news items, you can access them from this mobile app using the "cloud" feature. If this is your first time using any Kindle-type collections, then you can also search for items from the main login screen interface.

Use case: Library patrons are now, or soon will be, accessing content from a variety of mobile devices. One of the most popular places to purchase and access electronic books is the Amazon website. With Amazon pushing the book-buying market to adopt its hardware, your library users may be accessing Kindle books. Your library may be in the process of circulating Kindles to your users—after they return their Kindle checkout, they may want continued access to any items they have purchased with their Amazon account. In order to provide ongoing access to the contents of their e-books, the library can promote the use of the Kindle mobile app, which provides device-based access as long as users want to access their e-books.

Alternative use case: Alternatively, there is the library as provider of consumer electronics. The Amazon Kindle e-book reader may work as a stand-in for your user base having to actually purchase a Kindle device. As with many mobile networked devices the pace of innovation and obsolescence is rather quick, so one way to prevent your user base from having multiple obsolete technologies would be to adopt one device, or a minimum of devices, to meet their reading, research, and access needs.

What you should know/more information about how it works: Integration of the app with your Kindle content is provisioned by way of your Amazon login, so you need to have one set up (an Amazon login) before you can start to even use the app. There may be features that you'll miss if you are an avid Kindle user—specifically any screen technology (like the smart paper stuff) is just not going to translate over to your mobile display—so if you are used to features like that, you may find that lengthy reading isn't quite going to be possible or perhaps not as user-friendly on this device. You actually are required to go to the Amazon website in order to purchase and then sync the contents of the e-books in the Kindle.

Apps like this to look out for in the future: Future mobile e-reader apps may begin to incorporate other openly available text online. Other innovations in this space may also include prompting suggestions based on location, and of course based on previous purchases across locations or sellers.

Consulted: https://itunes.apple.com/us/app/kindle-read-books-ebooks -magazines/id302584613?mt=8

LIBRARY OF CONGRESS

Screenshot:

Figure 4.26.   Library of Congress. The main interface of the tour of the Library of Congress gives a helpful overview of collections, exhibits, and locations in the building.

What it does: This is a virtual tour of the Library of Congress. It introduces users to some of the wonders of the library, including the following destinations: the Main Reading Room, the Great Hall, Exploring the Early Americas, Creating the United States, the Bible Collection, Thomas Jefferson's Library, and Minerva artwork. Each of these sections includes pictures and image content that show the user of the app interesting art, exhibits, and architecture. Each stop also includes an audio tour and a related links section, to connect users of the app to additional information for each virtual tour stop.

Use case: For those library patrons interested in learning more about the world's largest library and collection, this virtual tour will serve as an engaging starting point for learning about the history, art, facilities, and collection of the Library of Congress. The app itself could be a good companion for users who are visiting the library and want to supplement their experience with a virtual tour as well.

Additional use case: Since the audio tour offers an introduction to the resources of the Library of Congress, it makes sense to make use of the audio portion for vulnerable populations—those who are unable to see a screen, or may not be able to read the smaller print of a mobile device.

What you should know/more information about how it works: This app achieves its rich tour experience through a couple of different media. For the first organizational effect the sections are arranged in a broad sectional overview, but the app is not overwhelming, since as you drill into the sections you are more interested in, the app then presents the detailed and annotated images of the area. For those who want to hear the audio tour, the audio is easily categorized here as well. The link to the Library of Congress website is useful.

Apps like this to look out for in the future: Cultural institutions are making significant inroads into providing compelling on-site and distance mobile applications. The future of these services may encompass aspects of location services or even augmenting your own experience in the library with graphical-informative overlays, through the camera's video feed.

Consulted: https://itunes.apple.com/us/app/library-congress-virtual -tour/id380309745?mt=8

MENDELEY REFERENCE MANAGER

Screenshot:

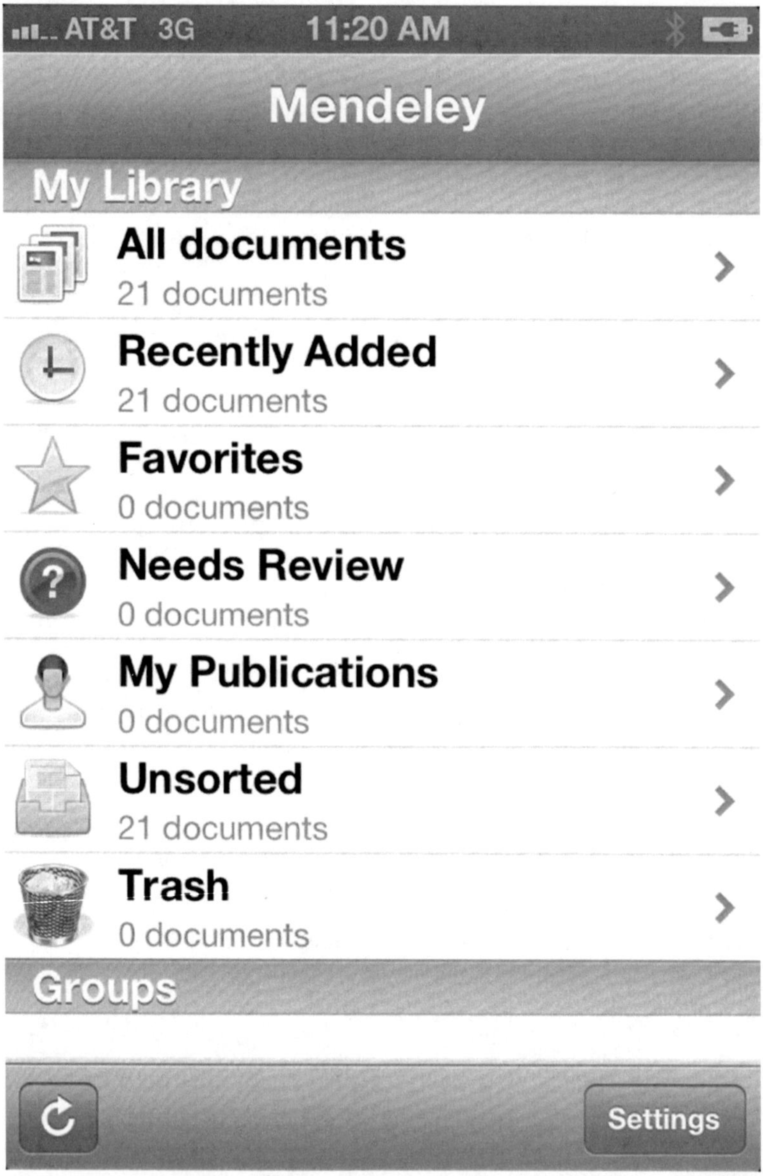

Figure 4.27. Mendeley Reference Manager. The reference manager will help users organize and get an overview of all of their saved citation from one easy-to-understand homescreen.

What it does: The Mendeley app provides mobile access to your saved references. You can read your saved PDFs offline as well. This resource gives you on-the-go access to your citations and allows you to add citations while away from your desktop computer.

Use case: Librarians at the research desk may want to recommend this app to the struggling graduate school student. These students have an overwhelming number of resources, and keeping all their citations in one place is ever more challenging considering the number of devices a student may be researching from. A graduate student may be at a lecture and want to record the citation mentioned; this app can help the student keep track of the citation and add it to their list of references. Sometimes recording a citation is not the problem—the real issue for the student is collecting all gathered citations and keeping them organized in one place, under one project folder. The Mendeley app will offer this organization and access to the student's total research portfolio. Such research optimization will lead to a highly efficient graduate student who can concentrate now solely on the business of writing.

What you should know/more information about how it works: It's a new type of bibliographic citation tool; if you've seen tools like RefWorks or End-Note, you kind of have a sense for how to understand a resource like this. Mendeley also allows sharing among collections and collaborators. This is a web-based resource, so there is no need for institutional subscriptions.

Apps like this to look out for in the future: Organization and management in the digital era does not become easy because of digital access. As a tool like Mendeley indicates, being able to cite media and other digital objects will be an important next step; the fragility of digital data is an important consideration, since a resource from the digital realm may not be available in the same fashion that scholarly content will be available. Apps such as these in the future will need to be able to capture and preserve the digital resource as much as organize it into the set of resources for a research project. Note also that bibliographic citation management is poised to become more social, mimicking the trend in science for increasingly collaborative work.

Consulted: http://www.mendeley.com/download

MINT.COM PERSONAL FINANCE

Screenshot:

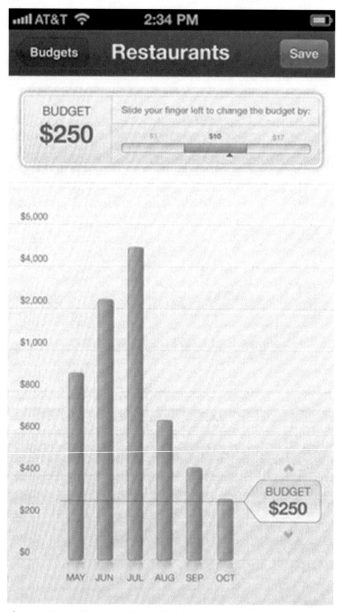

Figure 4.28. Mint.com. The mobile interface for Mint.com makes it simple to track your personal budget and meet savings goals as well.

What it does: This software tool is the mobile version of the free budget-keeping and personal finance management tool. You can load in your credit card statements, loan statements, investments, and savings or checking account information. From here you are able to create savings goals, track upcoming bills, and also understand, by way of Mint's analysis software, where your money has been spent over time. Creating budgets and tracking your progress is easy with this personal finance tool, and it features integration with the popular desktop-accessed tool as well.

Use case: Finance questions abound in public reference questions. Usually our patrons are searching for tools related to personal budgeting and general business-like questions. While librarians may have suggested websites in the past that could have served as resource points for personal budgeting, a mobile app tool such as Mint.com is well suited for the personalized features it can provide with regard to keeping a budget, managing bills, and creating and managing personal finance goals.

Additional use case: An additional use case for mobile applications that manage personal finance include aggregating all financial feeds into one interface. These include loans, credit card statements, and savings.

What you should know/more information about how it works: The app works by integrating with bank feeds or feeds from other financial institutions. The app functionality makes most sense if you log in and configure these feeds by desktop first. You are only required to make these connections an initial time by using Mint.com and secure authentication to your financial institutions. Once these accounts are linked you are able to get a global picture of your total finances and expenditures. One of the great value-adds for a service such as this is that Mint.com offers a classification and analysis of your total expenditures, so that you can graphically see how and where you are spending your money across all of your accounts.

Apps like this to look out for in the future: Future apps that connect with your personal finance will likely include new hardware and transmission affordances. These are going to enable the possibility for wallet-like payments using your phone as a payment conduit. Google has done some experimentation in this area, but apps that are using mobile payments are still in the early stage of development.

Consulted: https://itunes.apple.com/us/app/mint.com-personal-finance/id300238550?mt=8

MONSTER.COM JOB SEARCH

Screenshot:

Figure 4.29. Monster.com. Search results for a specific job type can be pushed to your mobile phone as more positions get added.

What it does: With Monster.com Job Search, you can access the content of the Monster.com Job Search website. As is standard on many contemporary mobile applications, this app includes the push notification feature. With the Job Search app you also have the ability to search, email, or apply for the job from the Monster.com platform. If you have created a profile in the desktop website in the past then you can re-use the login in the mobile app.

Use case: Librarians have seen an increase in the number of job-seekers and out-of-work patrons in the library. Certainly part of the librarian's job will be to point out any number of resources that could help patrons apply for jobs. With the app's push notifications when user-created filters are met, you can apply for jobs that fit your expertise almost instantly. Having the ability to browse jobs, save them to email, and look at them later, on your desktop, is a key use case here, too.

What you should know/more information about how it works: The real value to an app such as this is the interconnection between the desktop version and the mobile app version. The mobile display is easy to read through, and so searching for jobs is made quick and convenient in this app.

Apps like this to look out for in the future: Actually having your resume pre-loaded into the Monster.com website is a nice strategy, but a mobile device that allows you to upload, by way of an app, any resume to any site—not just Monster.com—will make for the greater number of uses and users.

Consulted: http://career-services.monster.com/mobile-apps/home.aspx

NOOK BY BARNES & NOBLE

Screenshot:

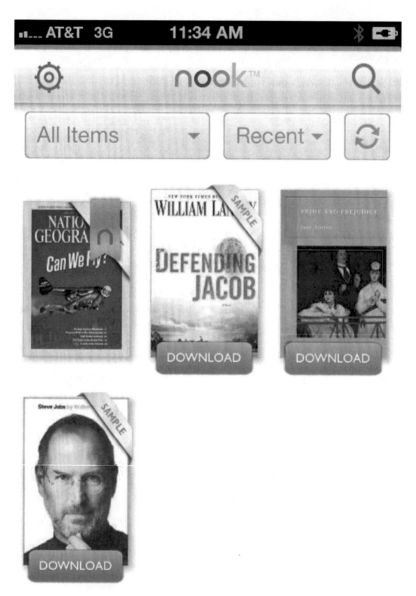

Figure 4.30.   Nook by Barnes & Noble. Viewing all of your items and book images is easy with the home screen's visual display of your e-books.

What it does: This Nook app provides cloud-based access to the titles you purchased through the Barnes & Noble website for access from the Nook device. The Nook app also keeps track of your last-read page on any device so that when you open a Nook e-book from your phone, you can pick up on the last page that you read on your Nook device. This also works if you are reading from your desktop computer and the mobile device.

Use case: The nice thing about a first-time startup of the current version Nook app by Barnes & Noble is that it comes preloaded with sample e-books to try out. Your library system could provide workshops for library patrons who are interested in purchasing e-book readers but aren't sure about how the content looks and how to download material. While one option for your patrons would be to visit a Barnes & Noble store, the library could provide an alternative means of learning about how the device formats e-books before a patron actually purchases a Nook device.

What you should know/more information about how it works: In order to sign in to the app on first load, you need to get a Barnes & Noble password. You can create a login at BN.com—it is free and easy to get set up. The full content of Barnes & Noble is not actually searchable from the Nook mobile app. The library user needs to first go to the Barnes & Noble website in order to download content. The search feature from this app searches content/e-books already in your Nook library. Your Nook library is associated with you by your BN.com login, so wherever you use that login (on the Nook or on the Nook mobile app), that is where your Nook library will be.

Apps like this to look out for in the future: The trend of mobile e-readers doesn't seem to be getting any less complicated. There is an increasingly diverse array of devices and platforms. A software tool such as a mobile app can help to reduce the strain that owning multiple devices may place on either your budget or your attention resources. If a new e-reading device comes along that does not seem to offer a companion mobile app for viewing on your phone, then perhaps one may want to pass on this— since the management of multiple devices is high cost.

Sources: https://itunes.apple.com/us/app/nook-by-barnes-noble/id373 582546?mt=8

NPR NEWS APP

Screenshot:

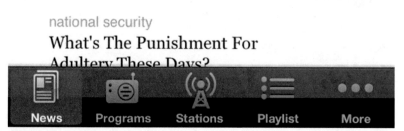

Figure 4.31.   NPR News. The simple list view makes it easy to discover and listen to or read top new stories.

What it does: With the NPR News app you are able to listen to news stories from NPR, listen to on-demand podcasts, and also make playlists of various news stories of interest to you, in the order you want to listen. The tabbed options at the bottom of the app interface allow you to choose news stories to read, or, alternatively, you can select from your favorite NPR programs to listen to the latest program. The app also shows which programs listed are currently "on air," so you have the option to listen to on-air programs through the app.

Use case: Traditional library browsing of periodicals can be supplemented with loaned iPads in the library browsing area. On these iPads (or other tablet devices), the library staff can load various news-reading apps. This mobile application by NPR is most likely to be one of the more sought-after and useful mobile news applications. The library will likely want to make a set of headphones available so that library users can listen to NPR programs and playlists without disturbing other library users.

Additional use case: For librarians there may be reference desk–facing uses, such as loading this app onto the iPad for on-duty reference librarians, or back office cataloging staff can stay current on news items that would be useful for day-to-day reference work or collection development.

What you should know/more information about how it works: The playlist feature functions much like the playlist options on your iPod, but rather than adding individual songs, this feature allows you to pick from an individual program's news stories so that you can mix and match the different stories that are of interest to you, even if they are not all from the same source.

Apps like this to look out for in the future: The ever-popular NPR is innovating quickly in this domain. The layout and functionality of the NPR News app is replicated in the NPR Music app, which the people at NPR are also focused on pushing out.

Consulted: http://itunes.apple.com/us/app/npr-news/id324906251?mt=8

ONENOTE

Screenshot:

Figure 4.32. OneNote. The home screen from the One-
Note app above indicates functionality in the bottom bar
module screen where a user can access notebooks and add
new notes to their folder system as well.

What it does: This is the mobile-accessible version of the Microsoft program OneNote, a place for storing and organizing notes and collabora-
tions. To begin using the OneNote app, you will need to log in with your
Windows Live ID. If you haven't ever used a Windows Live ID, you can
surf over to the login.live.com website and use your current email address as the Windows Live ID—make certain you click through the terms

of use agreement or else you won't be able to log in. Make notes using the phone's microphone to voice; the app also features integration of the camera portion of your smartphone so that you can take images and insert images into your notes.

Use case: Taking images and annotating these images may prove useful in certain research-like situations. A librarian may be touring the facilities of her library and wish to make improvements or notes on the physical plant. I often snap images with my iPhone and send them to maintenance departments. This may be an app that can keep track of your thinking for facilities upgrades and additional planning for facilities projects. If you already work in an area where you are satisfied with everything the library offers, facilities-wise, you may wish instead to catalog aspects of the successful layout of your library to showcase to potential patrons—as a sort of marketing strategy. You can take the images/make notes on them, and then email your notes to your desktop for further action at a later time.

Additional use case: Tablet uses of the OneNote app: the iOS version of OneNote can be loaded onto a library iPad. The device could be kept at a reference desk, or even shared among a team of instructional librarians. If there was cross-pollination among the reference team and instructional teams, the reference side of the operation could post notes on teaching that they've done at the desk and the instruction librarians could incorporate these techniques or common problems into their instructional sessions. The OneNote app supports information sharing and these items could also be emailed to the group if it turns out that not all teams are working at a single service point throughout the week.

What you should know/more information about how it works: Some of the features of the OneNote app will be familiar to users of the desktop system. The value-add will be synchronization of the note features between your desktop system and the mobile device. The app will also work on an iPad, and the developers have worked to incorporate design considerations that make creating and organizing notes on tablets easy and understandable, essentially making the user productive in the arena. The menu and tabbed viewing help make the app mobile-friendly.

Apps like this to look out for in the future: Microsoft software is fairly ubiquitous in the desktop realm. In the future the integration of these software components with mobile data should become more commonplace.

Consulted: https://itunes.apple.com/us/app/microsoft-onenote/id410395 246?mt=8

OPERA MINI WEB BROWSER

Screenshot:

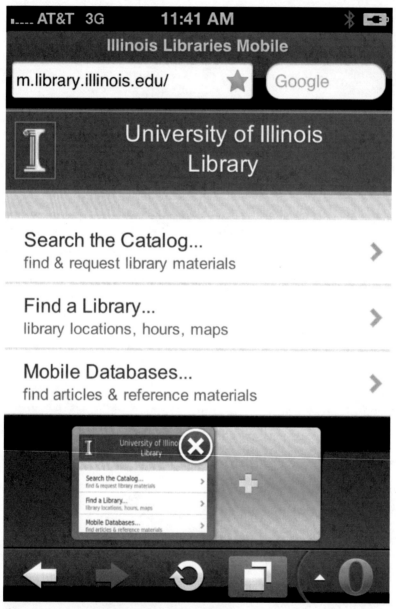

Figure 4.33.   Opera Mini Web Browser. The browser interface allows the user to have multiple tabbed browsing options.

What it does: Opera Mini is pitched as the data-light way to browse mobile web content. This app is really useful because it will work on numerous types of phones that have data plans, so it isn't just a browser for the iPhone or the Android devices. The fact that it keeps track of data received could help you to understand the rate your phone is using precious data plan minutes. The feature "Data Usage" is also an Opera Mini marketing tool, since it advertises itself as a potentially money-saving browser, but this also depends on how you use the app.

Use case: As part of a program in which librarians want to suggest alternative browsers to users, the mobile browser Opera Mini may be the tool to recommend for content that is mobile-formatted. Librarians will also want to ask users what it is that they do not like about their current mobile browser. This way they could better understand if their web-browsing needs might be answered by the Opera Mini Browser, which does seem to have a few integrated features that, depending on the user, can make for a replacement of default browsers.

Additional use case: For users who don't have a smartphone, the Opera Mini Browser would be a good way to search through content in a browser that is better suited for connecting to some of the web's more popular content, such as online commenting pages like Twitter or Facebook. The settings of the Mini Browser can be adjusted such that images are held back and not displayed in the browser. Of course this isn't the cutting edge of mobile technology capabilities, but it is an important use case for those who may not have access to the latest, or even any, smartphone technology.

What you should know/more information about how it works: The underlying technology of the Opera Mini Browser is to optimize for mobile display. This involves certain processing functions in the back-end of the system—these specifically include making use of compression servers which will pass data that is significantly smaller in size than normal desktop-based browsing.

Apps like this to look out for in the future: Low-tech solutions in mobile aren't necessarily the norm. The growth area for this type of app is probably slim. What we are more likely to see is the proliferation of more affordable smartphones, and even potentially a data plan affordability scale such that the barriers of entry for those on a tight budget will not be as high as they are now.

Consulted: http://www.opera.com/mobile/features/; http://itunes .apple.com/us/app/opera-mini-web-browser/id363729560?mt=8

POPSCI.COM

Screenshot:

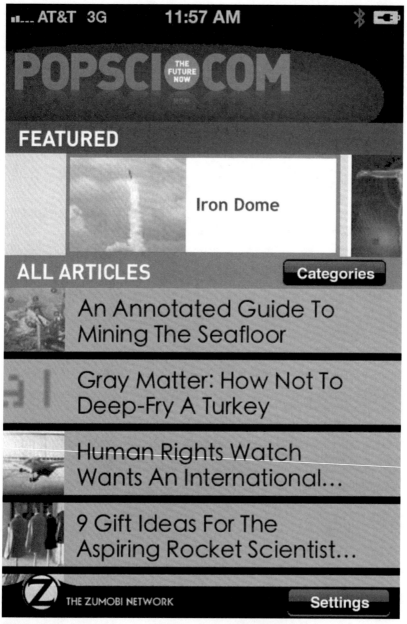

Figure 4.34. PopSci.com. Magazine browsing in mobile interfaces is made enjoy-able and interactive by the use of compelling visual design choices and well-placed images for stories.

What it does: This is an app for reading the content of the PopSci news website (popsci.com). The content of the app includes media and articles from the PopSci website. Within the app, the settings tab allows you to set up integration between what you are reading here and your Twitter or Facebook feeds. This app also allows you to filter by article category so that you can just be shown the content that is of immediate interest to you. Categories that are available include cars, environment, gadgets, science, and technology. The app features an easy-to-understand visual layout grid for stories, where the user can swipe through headings at the top of the app screen and then also pan through a list view of their selected category of interest.

Use case: The target audience for this in your library will be librarians, and those in the patron base who want to find accessible and leisurely science reading that is interesting and enjoyable to read. If you are looking to push out more interesting collections from your library Twitter account, you can consider linking from your library Twitter feed and then pushing out to followers or to your personal or professional Facebook timeline. In pushing out mobile technology tips or items of interest from your library Twitter feed, you may be able to reach out and connect with users who are more technically inclined and may not have been traditionally interested in library collections or services.

Alternative use case: As an additional use case of the PopSci app, consider its use in a tablet loaded with media content for leisurely reading. Library collections may be able to get retooled and refocused for tablet browsing. This may be a new area for what libraries have traditionally considered their leisurely browsing area.

What you should know/more information about how it works: This mobile app is basically the content of the PopSci.com website. The value-add for mobile on this one is that users could download articles to their mobile devices for offline reading, which is useful in areas without access to data or if it is necessary to preserve the data allowance of the mobile device data plan. For those users with an iPad, there is a larger, more visually interesting and compelling iPad app that more closely mimics the magazine-like viewing experience.

Apps like this to look out for in the future: The innovation in this app stems from the use of easy-to-understand graphical layout of the app home screen. Further, the interaction on the app and the horizontal and vertical panning from within make it easy to use and browse over. Future media-based apps that feature design like this will increasingly make use of the visual affordances in mobile. It makes sense to expect that apps of the future, in this vein, will actually offer a more compelling visual experience, especially as it relates to tablet-based media viewing.

Consulted: http://itunes.apple.com/app/popsci.com/id327916625?mt=8

PULSE

Screenshot:

Figure 4.35. Pulse. An exciting new development in news aggregators is the visual panning and scrolling options that Pulse is developing.

What it does: Pulse is an exciting news aggregator app. The name "news aggregator" may sound a bit off-putting, but in reality the visual appeal of this service helps to make it one of the most popular apps currently available for viewing news stories and providing up-to-date news feeds from popular news-type webpages. The user of the Pulse app can scroll vertically to select a news source, and then scroll horizontally to see stories within that news source. The news aggregator is customizable to news sources of your own interest, so you can add and remove areas as suits your reading preferences.

Use case: Library patrons have long browsed magazine shelves for leisurely and new reading; with this app, libraries would be able to configure a Pulse icon on a library iPad and put out a collection of Pulse titles that are relevant to a certain theme. The librarian who develops Pulse collections may leave one in the teen section of the library, and one near newspapers, while yet another may be placed around the media/current DVD section for entertainment-related information.

What you should know/more information about how it works: The Pulse app supports integration with and posting to social networks.

Apps like this to look out for in the future: The real value-add for an app like this is that it maintains what is interesting and useful about magazine browsing in the mobile app experience. This app is visually interesting to use and navigate, and it provides a great interface to multiple aggregated views of news sources. With its configurable feeds it looks to be one of the best new ways to view aggregated news on a mobile tablet.

Consulted: http://itunes.apple.com/us/app/pulse-news-for-iphone/id377594176

QUORA

Screenshot:

Figure 4.36. Quora. With a user-generated commenting and expert consulting forum system, the Quora boards are a great place to follow and learn more about interests you care about.

What it does: The mobile version of the popular question-and-answer page edited and organized by participants. This can supplement traditional desktop reference services in a crowd-source-type way.

The mobile version of Quora supports integration with your Facebook or Twitter account. The app allows access to the answering and posting of questions within the Quora community forums, with an "add question, create board, or post to board" module that supports searching and adding questions. Signing in with your Twitter or Facebook account helps to provide seed data for questions that you may be interested in based on what your followers/friends like.

Use case: If your library has a Twitter account, you can seed your followers for a Quora account based on what your community is interested in. From here, you could monitor user interest on your reference services iPad.

Additional use case: The new updates feature. If you wanted to engage your library patron base, perhaps an engaged group like tech aficionados, one thing you could do is create alerts and monitor from the mobile device when these tech individuals post to forums of relevance to your library. If they have a collection request, reference request, or some other library inquiry you can use Quora as a space to answer. This would be a public kind of forum, and since you have set the library tablet device to send updates, any time reference staff is on the desk, they can be notified of incoming questions or conversations around a topic.

What you should know/more information about how it works: Granted the crowd-sourced paradigm is a little different than the traditional top-down ask-a-librarian-a-query-and-expect-an-answer-type of work that classical librarianship comprises. If you and your library staff are comfortable with the idea of such things as Wikipedia, then Quora can be thought of as Wikipedia with a social aspect.

Apps like this to look out for in the future: In the future crowd-sourced information will of course center around conversation and other social networks as well.

Consulted: http://itunes.apple.com/us/app/quora/id456034437?mt=8; http://www.quora.com/

REDBOX

Screenshot:

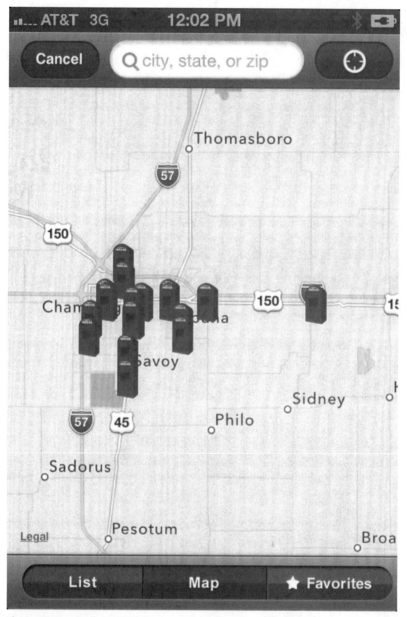

Figure 4.37.   Redbox. Find the nearest Redbox locations based on your current location.

What it does: For those of you who haven't made use of the Redbox stations outside of stores, the basic concept is that you can walk up to this station, peruse the contents, and walk away with a movie you rent. It is low cost, and because of the proximity to any given store, convenient. Redbox can essentially replace your trip to the video rental store. Its selection is limited, however, which is where the Redbox mobile app comes into play. The Redbox mobile app can tell you the collection contents of the Redbox near you. In addition you can search for "nearest Redbox" locations by using the Redbox app, which uses your GPS coordinates to identify the nearest Redbox.

Use case: Library services that dovetail with the Redbox renting platform could work in cooperative ways. As an example, consider that although any given library collection will have its strengths, it also will have gaps. In essence there may be areas of the collection that could be supplemented with the Redbox offerings. The mobile app could come in useful particularly for new feature film releases that your library does not include in its collection—or a popular title that the library may not have nearly enough copies of. With the mobile app library staff could identify kiosks that have titles that are nearest to their location, and library patrons could still get the item they need. This could help supplement the traditional reference sources one consults when identifying media items.

Additional use case: Redbox includes game rentals as well. Some libraries have started to collect in the gaming area, but for those that want to supplement or otherwise provide an additional option to their users in extending their gaming resources, identifying other RedBox stations in their community areas could help them access sought-after gaming titles. Patrons can reserve identified titles from a mobile device running the RedBox app.

What you should know/more information about how it works: In order to identify the RedBox locations in your area you need to allow the app to use your current location. Additionally, in order to place those reservations you need to either have a RedBox account or create a RedBox account. You can sign up from the app if you need to create a RedBox account.

Apps like this to look out for in the future: Libraries have been in the media-collecting sphere for some time, but providing the streaming content of media hasn't always been a library service. As new high-speed fiber comes into municipal offerings, it may be possible to stream more and more digital content to users' mobile devices assuming they are connecting to a service that has high-speed throughput.

Consulted: https://itunes.apple.com/us/app/redbox/id339532909?mt=8

SCIVERSE SCIENCEDIRECT

Screenshot:

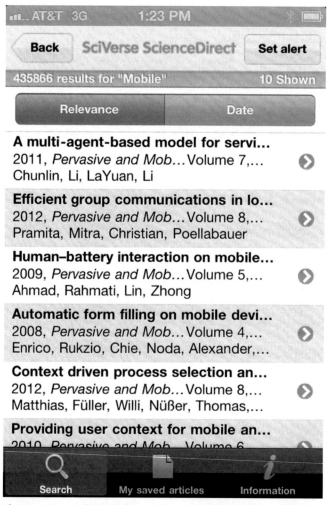

Figure 4.38. SciVerseScienceDirect. Search results in this important resource can be organized by either relevance or date of publication.

What it does: The SciVerse ScienceDirect app is a free download, but it works to provide individuals with the content that the institutions (home library accounts) have subscribed to. In addition to accessing the content of your subscription you can also use the ScienceDirect app to send articles by email. Essentially the app works to support the standard platform expectation you have when you are searching the ScienceDirect content. The app home screen is organized into three simple modules: a search tab, a saved articles tab, and an information tab. The information tab includes a helpful frequently asked questions page.

Use case: This app could be useful to library users, particularly those who are away from their home library, and perhaps away from their laptop, but need access to their research tools from a distance. A user in an airport who loads up the SciVerse app could make use of a known article search from the airport; you could also use the app on-the-go to see recent articles that have been published in a journal indexed here. Further, users have the option of saving articles to the app (by way of their user account) so they could theoretically use their travel downtime to scan the content they thought was previously interesting. This app will probably not replace standard desktop-based research workflows, but it will certainly keep busy researchers connected to the resources they need.

Additional use case: An additional use case of this app would be for users who do not have institutional subscriptions but would still like to search the contents of the SciVerse platform. This is possible with the permissions associated with "guest" level access accounts. Simply fill in your account information from the desktop-based website to obtain credentials. These credentials will allow guest accounts.

What you should know/more information about how it works: You have to register with SciVerse ScienceDirect on its website to get a username and ID—this has to be done before you can make use of any of the app functionality. The database connection does seem to get buggy at times, but a really helpful addition to the functionality of this app is an autocomplete tool that is preloaded with journal titles. This will save the users' time while typing on the mobile device screen, especially if they are not using any sort of Bluetooth-connected keyboard or do not have a device with a full built-in keyboard. Previous author searches are also saved in the app for your convenience. It will be easier to get back to your previous searches this way.

Apps like this to look out for in the future: Library apps by vendors don't quite reach the level of design experience and design performance app users would want to see in mobile apps. It may be that as other mobile app companies produce easier-to-use mobile apps, vendors will either learn to compete in this marketplace or begin to partner with third-party app developers that can deliver a visually compelling experience and make available the valuable data that libraries have come to rely upon.

Consulted: https://itunes.apple.com/us/app/sciverse-sciencedirect -free/id430923193?mt=8

SPARKNOTES

Screenshot:

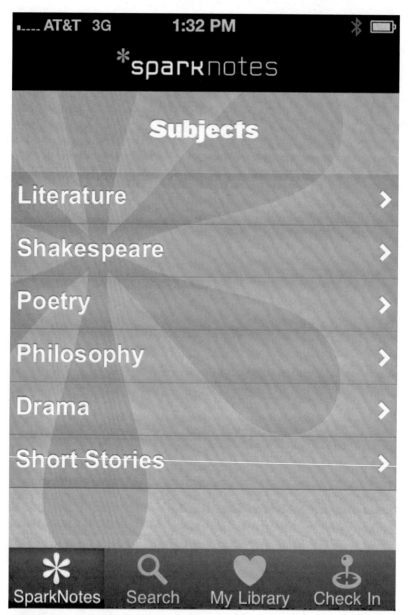

Figure 4.39.   SparkNotes. Selection of categories is made easy by the simple list view display in the homescreen.

What it does: The SparkNotes mobile app is the educational app that provides quick summaries of popular and classic texts. The app allows you to search by author, or title, for a SparkNotes report. The app main menu is organized by subject so that users can browse through the sections if they do not have a known title or author they want to search.

Use case: Users of the app may be from a few different user populations in your library; one of the most obvious use cases for this is among your young adult population. The content of these guides is well suited to mobile access and mobile reading. Young adult students may be more interested in learning from these small, micro-sized chunks of information rather than accessing entire e-books from their mobile devices. In this way, connecting with the young adult population of your library makes most sense for this content.

Additional use case: Another useful way to make use of this app in a library setting would be for advising readers what next to read. Any user population that is interested in learning about the next book they may want to read can use the app to read a synopsis of the plot or about the characters, or learn more information about the author, if that is important for them.

What you should know/more information about how it works: This app asks to use your current location, so that you can check in and share what you are reading and where you are reading it. Another thing to keep in mind about this mobile app is the functionality to download a chapter to the app to read later. This will be important for the user with limited data, or, alternatively, for users in areas without data coverage for extended periods of time.

Apps like this to look out for in the future: This reformatting and new media adaptation of a popular and sought-after educational resource would seem to indicate that the quick, easy to understand help guides used in education may be coming to mobile apps. If there are concise reference-type sources in education be on the lookout for these to be reformatted to the mobile app area.

Consulted: http://itunes.apple.com/us/app/sparknotes/id506427167?mt=8

SKYDRIVE

Screenshot:

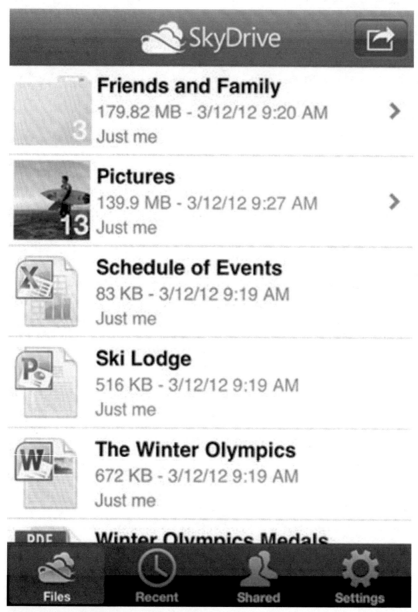

Figure 4.40.   SkyDrive. The drive provides access to all your media items and types from a simple file organizing home screen.

What it does: This is Microsoft's storage solution—where you can look at and manage your files while on a mobile device. It is similar in concept to services like Google Drive and Dropbox (cloud storage on the go). Those who own Windows phones will be able to open and use the files from their mobile device. The app supports photo upload directly into the Sky-Drive app from the iPhone.

Use case: File sharing on the go is sometimes cumbersome—especially if the file you need isn't accessible from your mobile phone, and oftentimes it really isn't. Sometimes you'll need a Word document, but other times you may want to consult and edit an Excel file with budgeting or tracking data inside. Unless you've already chosen a cloud-based solution, editing this file is not straightforward. SkyDrive from Microsoft will allow you to open your files, make edits, and then send these on to your collaborators; being able to do all of this on the go does help you be more efficient and save time because you do not have to locate a desktop system that can access your files.

Additional use case: The app offers image upload that connects with your already-existing Microsoft files/projects. For librarians working in primarily Microsoft shops, it may make sense to load roving systems with the SkyDrive software in order to share and collaborate from service points; documents can be added to these service areas with the help of image input from the iPad or even iPhone. Librarians can also email any updates to a group staff-facing email account.

What you should know/more information about how it works: Because it is a Microsoft product you will need a Microsoft Live ID in order to log in and make use of the app functionality.

Apps like this to look out for in the future: As Microsoft continues its attempt to make inroads into the mobile phone market, it will leverage the desktop dominance of office tools. The close nature of the platform may be prohibitive for many, since gaining a Live ID is a barrier to quickly making use of an app. It doesn't seem on first glance that apps like this in the future will be more open or amenable to users outside the sphere of Microsoft's influence.

Consulted: http://itunes.apple.com/us/app/skydrive/id477537958?ls=1 &mt=8

TED

Screenshot:

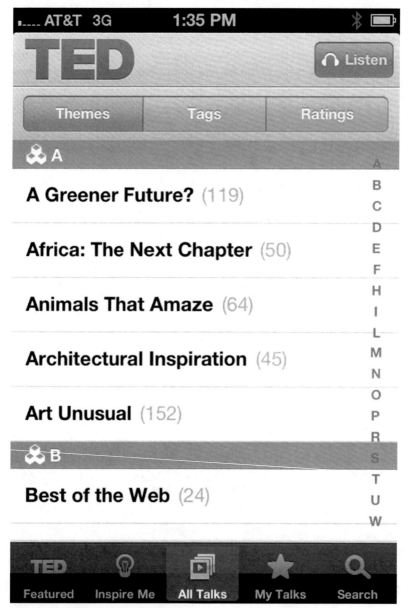

Figure 4.41.   TED. The three-panel tab bar at the top of the interface includes options for searching by themes, tags, or ratings.

What it does: TED is the "Technology, Entertainment, Design" suite of talks. This app provides the mobile video content of the popular and inspiring TED Talks. The mobile interface features the following modules: a featured section, organized by new and popular videos; "Inspire Me"—a random video player that guides you to "undiscovered talks"; and a section for all talks, organized by theme, tags, and ratings. The final two modules include a "My Talks" module organized by downloads and bookmarks, and a search option, so that you can do known-title searches over the collection of Ted Talks. There is also a listen button at the top of the app where you can listen to the NPR TED Talk radio hour, streaming to your mobile device.

Use case: Many people in the library world will have been positively impacted by the inspirational TED Talks. According to the iTunes App Store, users with an iPad can view TED Talk videos on demand. However, if you have an iPhone or an iPod Touch, you have to download the video you want to watch—it will not be immediately available for watching on the small devices (download or bookmark options are available here). So libraries with iPad collections should consider loading the TED Talks onto the mobile tablets, and the users will have instant access to the TED Talk library.

Additional use case: If your library environment is set up with a mobile browsing area or you allow your users to connect to live radio streams, this app could be useful for connecting to the TED Talk radio channel stream.

What you should know/more information about how it works: The streaming pretty much works on the iPhone, it just may vary based on connection speed and device; the recommendation to download rather than stream the video makes sense if you are on a wireless data plan, not on a Wi-Fi connection.

Apps like this to look out for in the future: The interesting thing about this app is that it doesn't even necessarily take advantage of the mobile affordances; it is kind of just a squeezed-down and light version of the website.

Consulted: http://itunes.apple.com/us/app/ted/id376183339?mt=8

TRIPADVISOR

Screenshot:

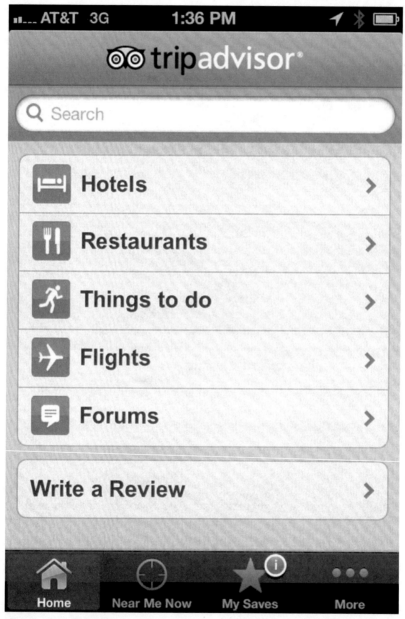

Figure 4.42.   TripAdvisor. The home screen displays search options by category and provides easy one-touch access to your saved results.

What it does: The TripAdvisor app provides your Android or iOS device mobile access to hotel reviews and travel information. You can search airfare deals as well as hotel booking information from the mobile interface. The main interface of the app is organized into a home screen with the following search options: hotels, restaurants, things to do, flights, and forums. You are also able to write a review for one of these from the home module. A "near me now" tab is the second main feature of the app, which uses your GPS coordinates to suggest places to stay, eat, or see. Finally, you are able to save your favorites in a "my saves" module, which stores all of your favorite places, hotels, and other stuff.

Use case: Actually consulting the user-generated and user-contributed feedback from the TripAdvisor app before visiting an unknown hotel will save your library patrons from travel destinations that are to be avoided or potentially below par. Consider also contributing reviews of restaurants or destinations in your patron community. This would be a fine way to help improve the quality of life in your area—visitors and those who live in your town alike will be well served by the content, which could help them navigate new and not-yet-tried locations around them.

Additional use case: You can make booking choices for housing or eating out based on the content in the reviews section, but an additional use case would be finding activities or events in a new area with the TripAdvisor app. Librarians may want to recommend this for new residents in the area, and in this way the library may actually help users find their way and experience new things in the community. Librarians may also find it a useful way to engage the community by submitting events or activities in the area.

What you should know/more information about how it works: The TripAdvisor app asks to use your current location. With the "near me now" tab, reviews and deals for destinations in your immediate surroundings will be displayed. If you don't want the TripAdvisor application to make suggestions to you based on your location, make sure to unselect the location-sharing feature when you first load the application.

Apps like this to look out for in the future: A similar type of consumer-facing product is UrbanSpoon, but the arena for user-contributed reviews is growing and sites like these can only continue to help consumers make informed choices. Future apps in the realm of user-contributed reviews are likely to be shaped around local needs and by local users.

Consulted: https://play.google.com/store/apps/details?id=com.trip advisor.tripadvisor; https://itunes.apple.com/us/app/tripadvisor-hotels -flights/id284876795?mt=8

URBANSPOON

Screenshot:

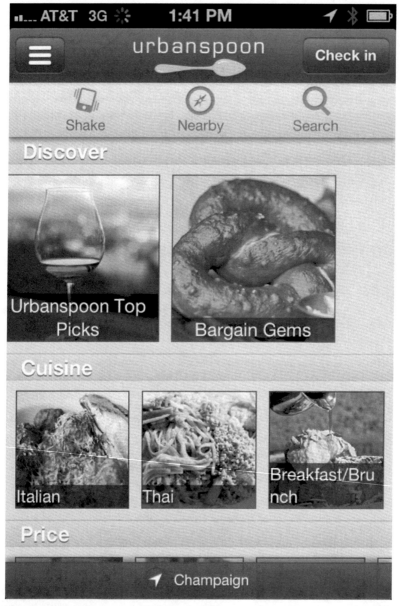

Figure 4.43.   Urbanspoon. The visual grid layout of search options makes this an intuitive, easy-to-understand interface.

What it does: On first load the Urbanspoon application gives three immediate options: "shake," "nearby," and "search." The interesting thing about the Urbanspoon mobile app is that we see on first load the affordances of mobile—just search by shaking the phone! But the app is also a platform for commenting on restaurants and getting suggestions for other places close to you to eat. That being said, you will want to be sure to enable your location sharing for the app, since having nearby places recommended is one of the advantages of the mobile app.

Use case: Library patrons are keen on bringing their own food into the library—this is allowed in certain places, and certain libraries also have built-in cafés. If you have an eating zone in your library an app like Urbanspoon could be advertised here, or even help those who want more substantial eating options to find nearby places to eat in your community.

What you should know/more information about how it works: You don't have to be near a restaurant in order to get recommendations; there is a search feature that can organize the results by distance.

Apps like this in the future: Locally submitted user content provided by way of mobile interfaces is an interesting development in social and commercial engagement. While users of this app will probably be in the library community, it may make sense to help local businesses understand how in the future the decisions that consumers make about purchases will be done increasingly on the go and using content that the business owners may not be able to control.

Consulted: https://itunes.apple.com/us/app/urbanspoon/id284708449 ?mt=8

USA TODAY NEWS

Screenshot:

Figure 4.44. *USA Today* **News. A simple list view paired with accompanying images and visuals for each article makes** *USA Today* **a compelling app for concise news.**

What it does: This is the newspaper content of the *USA Today* national newspaper. The app allows you to view media content from your mobile device. The familiar *USA Today* newspaper sections are available here: news, money, sports, life, tech, travel, and opinion, within which you can watch streaming video from a "top videos" section on the stories site. There is also an easy-to-pan-through "day in pictures" feature bundled with the app.

Use case: This news source can be for research or for leisurely reading for your library patrons. Since the *USA Today* app is also available for a number of tablet devices the software could work for an in-library tablet browsing area. Tablet kiosk viewing in a library setting could also be configured to provide access to the content of the *USA Today* app.

Additional use case: Alternatively, this app could be available for librarians at service points where they may be without desktop access—they would be able to quickly see and watch news from a librarian-issued tablet device.

What you should know/more information about how it works: On first load the *USA Today* app asks to send you push notifications. You can configure these push settings in the notifications settings the app will push out. You can also recommend and share stories on Facebook or Twitter with this app—emailing articles works from the app as well.

Apps like this to look out for in the future: One very interesting aspect of the *USA Today* app is the overlays that are instructional in nature—these instructional overlays are useful to those users who do not have much experience navigating a mobile apps screen. The functionality can be confusing on first impression, especially for those who primarily do computing on desktop systems.

Consulted: https://itunes.apple.com/us/app/usa-today-for-ipad/id3642 57176?mt=8

VEVO VIDEO STREAMING

Screenshot:

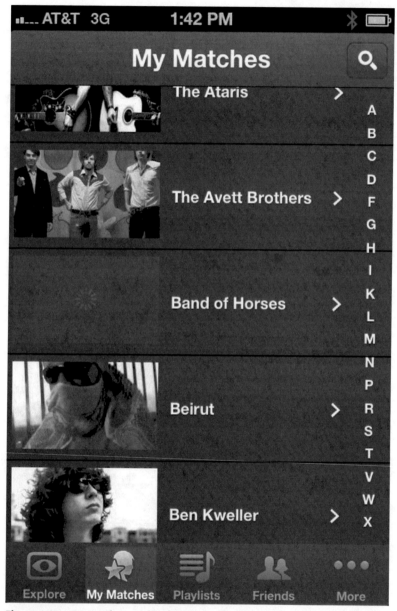

Figure 4.45. Vevo. The matches function will suggest and auto-populate lists of videos for users based on previous search and views.

What it does: Vevo is a music video streaming application. With Vevo your library's patrons, like students, or other librarians can access the music videos that they are interested in viewing from their mobile device. The Vevo app has a great visual display for browsing and viewing music videos of interest. Most users interested in contemporary musicians will find this resource valuable. The Vevo app is free but is supported by video ads before the video plays. There is also a social networking feature that allows you to publish music videos you watch to your Facebook timeline—this is an optional feature that you can turn on and off as it suits your needs.

Use case: Users interested in viewing streaming media on the go will be particularly well served by this resource. Picture the high school student visiting the public library. This student may want access to video collections that the library doesn't have access to in the catalog. An alternative to ordering contemporary videos or providing access to on-demand teen resources, the Vevo app can be a valuable reference resource for this cohort. Suggest the Vevo app to your clientele that needs access to streaming video in the library. The Vevo content can be delivered via your library WiFi connection to the phone, or via your patrons' own data plan.

Additional use case: Pair this app with the Shazam app, where users can identify a music video and then view additional, related video content from the Vevo application. These other music videos that are related to the user's initial query may help them discover new, useful content.

What you should know/more information about how it works: The Vevo app functions similarly to the web-based Vevo desktop version. The value-add for this app in being mobile is the ability to sign in to your account and retrieve your favorites from an already existing and set-up account. In the case that YouTube doesn't contain the music video content that you need, you may want to try a Vevo search, since the content here is only music videos, and the content of YouTube is much more expansive.

Apps like this to look out for in the future: Streaming video and other data-intensive tools will certainly challenge data providers and phone companies into the near future—apps like these may wane in popularity if data plans become prohibitively costly. However, specialty video-viewing apps such as Vevo are successful when they use easy-to-understand layouts, interaction, and prominent images in such a way that users can interact with content.

Consulted: http://itunes.apple.com/us/app/vevo/id385815082?mt=8; https://play.google.com/store/apps/details?id=com.vevo

WEBMD

Screenshot:

Figure 4.46.   WebMD. The mobile version of WebMD provides similar functionality to the desktop version.

What it does: The WebMD app for iPhone supports the functionality of the web-based health sites. In fact, if you have a WebMD login from the desktop where you have saved searches, information, or alerts, you can use it with the app. Many librarians are familiar with referring users with health-related queries to this page.

Use case: If community members in your library are new to the area, there is helpful location support within WebMD—the app helps users find their way to doctors' offices—with a mapping feature and directional support.

Additional use case: Alternatively, in library settings, users may prefer a more private or at least less public space to look up health-related information and symptoms. A mobile interface on the user's own personal device may be more suitable for such viewing.

What you should know/more information about how it works: The functionality of the app also supports helpful emailing tools, so you can send information to your email account from the app, to study later or even follow up with your doctor.

Apps like this to look out for in the future: Certainly early mobile development and uses started in the medical support area. For those librarians working in medical librarianship there may be additional innovative tools. These might include locating patients in buildings with mobile technologies or the reformatting of a number of medical-based resources, like databases, for viewing on tablets and phones.

Consulted: http://itunes.apple.com/us/app/webmd-for-ipad/id3731856 73?mt=8

WIKIPEDIA MOBILE

Screenshot:

Main Page

Today's featured article

Windsor Castle is a medieval castle and royal residence in Windsor in the English county of Berkshire, notable for its long association with the British royal family and for its architecture. The original motte-and-bailey castle, built after the Norman invasion by William the Conqueror, was designed to protect Norman dominance around the outskirts of London and to oversee a strategically important part of the River

Figure 4.47. Wikipedia Mobile. A familiar look and feel is one of the highlights for Wikipedia Mobile.

What it does: This is the mobile interface for the popular reference source Wikipedia. Users of the free Wikipedia app can search for quick facts and micro-sized chunks of information from their mobile device. The familiar iOS functionality of pinching and zooming in on images and other media content is maintained here.

Use case: The Wikipedia app can be used in a variety of situations, from quick factual information needs to getting started with key terms related to a research lead. What the Wikipedia app can support is the quick information need on the go—it probably will not serve your library users for definitive information or comprehensive overviews of a topic.

Additional use case: Another use case for the Wikipedia mobile app is the affordances of the app for computing and technical terms. Since the online community that edits Wikipedia has crafted these pages, the science and tech areas of Wikipedia are quite strong in this area. So when a patron needs access to a reference tool regarding computing or programming, and your library collection only has older books in the subject, consider pointing your user to the mobile Wikipedia page as a reference source for this area.

What you should know/more information about how it works: It appears the app is pulling content from a Wikipedia API, which makes it appear slower than the desktop-based Wikipedia you are familiar with.

Apps like this to look out for in the future: Popular reference sources are certainly first in line for mobile adaptation. An interesting development for Wikipedia will be the rate at which users begin to connect from their mobile interfaces to this user-generated and -curated reference tool. At present, the app features some of the common search functionalities users familiar with Wikipedia will expect, however, the production of articles from integrated image upload is not yet a possibility in this app.

Consulted: http://itunes.apple.com/us/app/wikipedia-mobile/id324715 238?mt=8

YAHOO! AXIS

Screenshot:

Figure 4.48.   Yahoo! Axis. This is a simple, easy-to-use integration of the Yahoo! Axis browser with other social networking platforms.

What it does: It is a web browser, and it is extremely well designed. The Yahoo! Axis mobile application supports web browsing and more on your mobile device. You may be wondering why it is necessary to have mobile app browsers as apps—the use cases for these shown below indicate that the swiping of the phone helps provide a visualization of search results that is better suited to mobile search and display. It lends itself to small-screen search. Typical mobile browsers only simulate the desktop search for mobile, whereas Yahoo! Axis is able to respond visually to the small-screen needs.

Use case: Searching and finding material quickly on the mobile web isn't easy. Librarians looking for a browser that they could use on their reference iPads may want to consider making use of the Yahoo! Axis app. It allows the librarian to pan to the left, under the search box, and filter by type of resource. The mobile faceting for images makes sense and is intuitive to make use of.

Additional use case: This app also supports tabbed browsing. You can select all of the browser's tabs from the tab button on the bottom of the browser window. This is useful for roving reference librarians who may have multiple pages opened on their iPad and want a way to quickly view the items in the tabs from a simple view.

What you should know/more information about how it works: Axis can make use of the push setting on the iPhone for alerts notification. Axis also has a local search feature that will use location to inform the results returned.

Apps like this to look out for in the future: Experimentation with the traditional list view of mobile design will likely progress in the future. Apps that favor the visual over the more mundane versions of mobile display will gain traction here. More and more, the Android platform is looking to create compelling visual elements as much as maintain their open source and open platform ethos. A guide to Android design styles is available here: http://developer.android.com/design/style/index.html.

Consulted: http://axis.yahoo.com/

YELP

Screenshot:

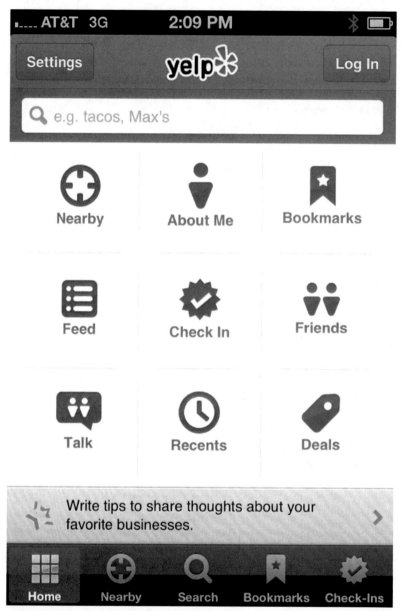

Figure 4.49.   Yelp. The grid icon layout makes it easy for users to understand functionality.

What it does: The popular business lookup and commenting tool comes to the mobile world with the Yelp Mobile app. From the mobile version of Yelp, you can access most of the standard functionality of the desktop version. This includes business lookups and reviews, but also some very helpful mobile features, like filtering your search results based on restaurants that are currently open and showing which ones are currently nearest to you. You can make reservations with the integrated OpenTable reservation tool. Also the app supports social network integration with Facebook timelines and Twitter feed integration from the "check in" tab of the app.

Use case: Librarians interested in community outreach and connecting patrons with local businesses will want to incorporate the Yelp app into their suggested resources. Librarian workshops can feature a small business consulting/business intelligence workshop to interested community members on how to integrate their small businesses' virtual space with the Yelp interface. Since most users on the go will be accessing the content of Yelp from a mobile device, it makes sense to introduce the mobile views of local businesses during such a workshop and explain functionality.

What you should know/more information about how it works: The Yelp app works from user-submitted feedback, as much as it does from business owners curating their home pages.

Apps like this to look out for in the future: Location sharing and local exploration are two interesting features and advantages to mobile. Libraries involved in their communities will want to watch this area as there may be opportunities to further integrate into communities and to help draw commerce to local businesses. The apps in the future that will look like Yelp will continue to build on the social networking–based content, but also, as a parallel development, will build on location features.

Consulted: https://itunes.apple.com/us/app/yelp/id284910350?mt=8

YOUSENDIT

Screenshot:

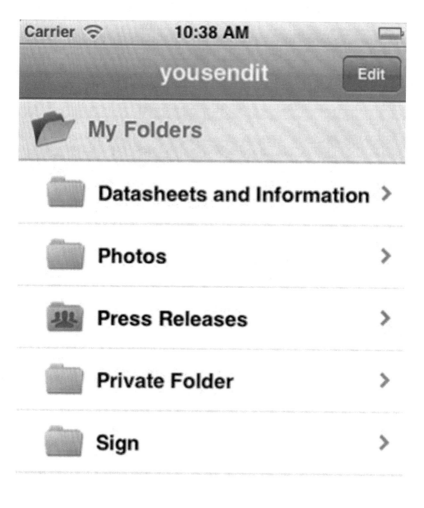

Figure 4.50.   YouSendIt. Managing and sharing large files is convenient with the mobile interface.

What it does: This is a file-sharing app that can store your documents, spreadsheets, and presentations in the cloud and help to facilitate sharing, especially if the documents are too large to send over email.

Use case: Like many of the file-sharing apps reviewed here, this one boasts cloud-based storage. The user of the YouSendIt app is likely to have already preconfigured their YouSendIt account from a desktop machine. The reason for this is that mainly you aren't going to be accessing very large files from your mobile phone anyway, and certainly, it isn't very easy to see the files you may have access to from a mobile phone. The YouSendIt app provides an easy way to view the contents of the files you have uploaded and made available to your collaborators through the cloud.

What you should know/more information about how it works: This app has a desktop version and becoming familiar with the desktop functionality can help to streamline your mobile interaction, or help you to retrieve files that you may have sent while you were on your desktop system.

Apps like this to look out for in the future: As storage continues to come down in price, apps and services like these will grow. The aspect of this arena to pay attention to is consideration of which apps you want to use to share your work with others. Perhaps an area of innovation will include the ability to share with whomever, regardless of the mobile service that is storing your files and other cloud-based content. Somewhere there has to be a single-point authentication in the future; will it continue to be the Facebook/Twitter combination or will something else come along and begin to be the go-to place of login credentials for sharing across apps?

Consulted: http://itunes.apple.com/us/app/yousendit/id442140135?mt=8

YOUTUBE

Screenshot:

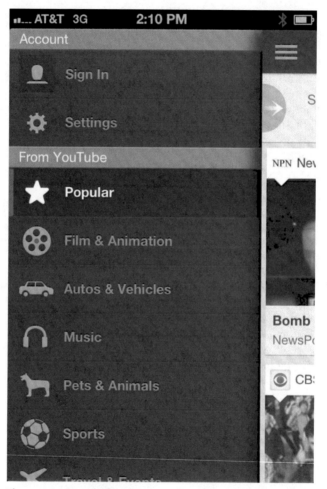

**Figure 4.51.   YouTube. There are a number of options in the
slide-out view within the YouTube interface.**

What it does: The most recent iOS version, version 6, was released as this
manuscript was going to print. With the release of this version, YouTube
is not a native app. For this reason, users will need to go to the iTunes
App store to download. The YouTube app for iOS 6 includes native app
viewing of the content of the YouTube library. You can also upload video
from the YouTube app as well.

Use case: Many library systems, from academic to public, have actually created YouTube channels for instructional, marketing, and outreach efforts. For library users, connecting from their mobile device to the library YouTube channel may be one of the quickest and easiest ways to connect with the library, but consider when making a video for your user population that a mobile channel may need different design considerations. These considerations may include writing video content that is short, using large text or sparing text, and making any graphics or icons large enough so that mobile device users will be able to understand them. You can make use of encoding techniques in the video creation portion of your work such that viewing on mobile will be easier for your end users, but these considerations need to be made up-front and the format that you upload the video for will need to be encoded for small-screen viewing.

Additional use case: Another way to use a YouTube app in a library setting is during library orientation efforts that are suited to patron creation of content. Consider an academic library orientation program where users (first-year students) are first tasked with shooting a video in the library with library-provided iPods (the 4th Generation iPod Touch devices have forward-facing cameras) and then they upload some of the content into a first-year-student channel/space within YouTube. Since first-year students are primarily learning about the university setting and library setting from each other, this can be an additional digital orientation for the new students, who can access the user-generated orientation material at their leisure.

What you should know/more information about how it works: The YouTube app also supports integration/sharing among the other social networks to which your library users may belong, the integrated posting to Facebook timelines, and Google Plus accounts. It offers a way to share and connect the content of the YouTube library offerings with the user's social networks. Many users may have also created subscriptions from their YouTube logins (Gmail account logins work for this), so the mobile YouTube app offers the subscribed content for users' accounts as well.

Apps like this to look out for in the future: Since YouTube is not a native app on iOS 6, librarians may be tasked with explaining to users that iOS devices after 2012 can play YouTube content from a mobile app interface, but in order to do so they must download it from the app store. Similar work-around techniques will need to be introduced for the mapping tool, which also saw a new update. Users may want to know where else they can find map-like Google features from a mobile interface, something that is yet to be determined in the early days of the iOS 6 system features.

Consulted: https://itunes.apple.com/us/app/youtube/id544007664?mt=8

ITUNES U

Screenshot:

Figure 4.52. iTunes U. The modular navigation within the app will be familiar to those users of the iTunes App Store.

What it does: This app is a platform that provides free course content from universities that contribute materials such as lectures and assignments. The app has a similar look and feel to the iTunes App Store, with courses that are featured as "staff picks," along with currently trending popular courses, and recently added content.

Use case: This app could be used by library patrons for continuing education or additional training in an area of interest. For those users of the library anticipating attending a variety of institutions, a platform like this could help prospective students make a decision about attending a university by way of looking at popular course content from that school.

What you should know/more information about how it works: Once you locate content that you are interested in, you can subscribe to the course and get updates as new lectures are available. Or, if you only want one or two lectures, you can just download the ones you like—in this way enrolling in a course is a little like subscribing to a podcast.

Apps like this to look out for in the future: There is considerable disruption in the higher education open learning space. The massive online open courses (MOOCs) have been some of the more popular in recent times, but apps that dovetail with or extend the MOOC movement will be an area to watch.

Consulted: https://itunes.apple.com/us/app/itunes-u/id490217893?mt=8

Chapter 5

Social Apps for Library Services

The mobile versions of common social networking tools can be used to connect with library patrons as well as librarians. Below a few of these are reviewed for their applicability to library services, collections, and library expertise. We'll talk here about Facebook, Twitter, and other mobile social apps and their potential application to library service.

AOL AIM

Screenshot:

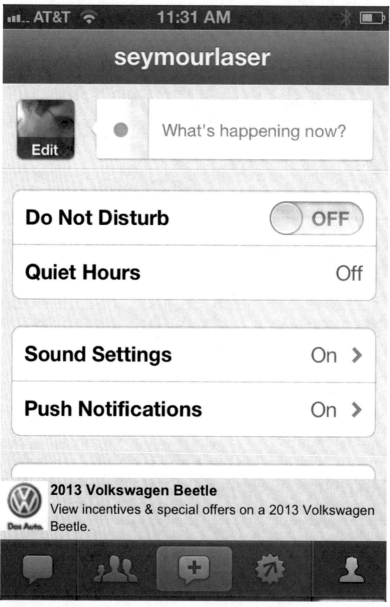

Figure 5.1.   AOL AIM. The instant messaging interface allows for simple configuration of mobile push notification and settings.

What it does: This app is the mobile app that provides on-the-go chat functionality for your instant messaging services. The app is able to aggregate feeds from your Facebook timeline as well, so you can receive up-to-date feeds from your social networks from the AOL app. In addition to this a deeper Facebook integration is evident here, since the app allows login with Facebook credentials. The user of this AOL AIM app is also able to use group chat functionality, which brings AIM into the social sphere.

Use case: The most common library use to recommend to your patron base is that your users have an AOL AIM app loaded onto their device if they want to quickly connect with your mobile reference service. As a part of your virtual reference services marketing you can let your users know that mobile reference can be SMS-based, but it can also be based in the traditional IM paradigm while on the go.

Additional use case: Your library staff may want to connect in the office with one another, which can be accomplished with IM chat. If your library staff is on the go, or lives in embedded office locations, it makes sense to employ an app such as this to facilitate keeping in touch or collaborating from different locations.

What you should know/more information about how it works: On first load the app asks to send you push notifications. The graphical layout of this app is quickly understood and nicely designed as well.

Apps like this to look out for in the future: Messaging apps that have come online recently and disrupted the mobile landscape are those apps that replace traditional text messaging services that are provided by carriers. Look for innovation in the area to replace some of the standard texting services on mobile devices.

Consulted: http.//itunes.apple.com/us/app/aim-free-edition/id2817045 74?mt=8

BUMP

Screenshot:

Figure 5.2.   Bump. By using your contacts lists you will be able to more quickly and easily share image content with devices without using Bluetooth.

What it does: You can link your social networking accounts such as Facebook, Twitter, and LinkedIn. Once you link any of the accounts to the app they become part of your business card, which gets exchanged with another user who has the Bump app enabled. You can also "bump" images to your computer with the app.

Use case: Librarians and other busy professionals rarely have time to catalog and organize business cards from conferences. With this app, two users who have the Bump app loaded simply bump their phones together to exchange virtual business cards. The app will store them into a contacts file and you will be able to connect with the bumped contact at a later time. This could be a real time-saver for those who either refuse to use business cards, or are unable to remember where they placed a new contact's business card.

Additional use case: You can also share images by way of the Bump app—this may be useful for library patrons to know about if they are concerned about transferring photos from one system to another. From your mobile device all you need to do is pan over to the "share photos" portion of the app, and then on your computer visit the Bump website. After you enable location sharing in the browser you will be able to connect your mobile phone with your laptop and share photos between the two devices by a bump of the device onto the keyboard.

What you should know/more information about how it works: The Bump app does not use Bluetooth at all; the bump is actually mapped from sensors in the phone using server-side algorithm matching. The location of the bump is included to narrow down the uniqueness of the bump to two phones.

Apps like this to look out for in the future: The Labs portion of the Bump company website indicates a bump-to-pay feature under development. Mobile e-payments are growing in importance, especially as the market moves from mobile advertising (still figuring this out) to mobile payments (some early adopters are innovating in this area already).

Consulted: http://itunes.apple.com/us/app/bump/id305479724?mt=8; http://bu.mp/company/faq

FACEBOOK

Screenshot:

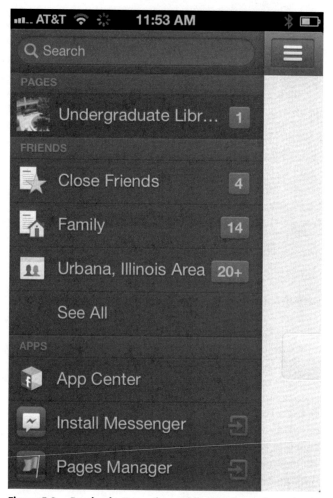

Figure 5.3. **Facebook. From the mobile interface of Facebook, you can post images or any updates to your library social presence.**

What it does: Connect to Facebook's social platform from any mobile device—Android or iOS. The new iOS version supports retina display for those users who require such resolution. You can upload images to your Facebook presence from the app, respond to messages, and also utilize the popular chat functionality of Facebook by way of the mobile app. It is also possible to update your status from the mobile app version of Facebook.

Use case: For the embedded librarian, reaching out to a population of users by way of social networking tools is an important facet of your position. This outreach includes being in the location where your users are. You can announce your presence to the clientele you serve by way of checking in to your embedded location. If there are specific offices or even specific buildings in which you want to announce your presence, make use of the Facebook mobile app in order to provide an announcement to your user base. This assumes that you are using a professional Facebook account that you link to your clientele from. From here your clients may even send you quick informational questions by way of Facebook messenger service, so you'll want to be able to respond to these on the go, if you happen to be between office locations or lack a standard desktop connection, which is possible in embedded-type settings.

Additional use case: A use case for the mobile version in public library settings would be to demonstrate mobile social networking affordances, which include uploading photos directly from your device, checking into places, and interacting with most of the content services directly from your mobile device. Of course the standard scavenger hunt around town by way of a public library paired with the mobile check-in service that the Facebook mobile app supports would be a fine way to both introduce users to the surrounding community and document these for later on the user's timeline, thus allowing the user to go back and investigate the places at a later time, while not forgetting any important locations.

What you should know/more information about how it works: Most of Facebook's functionality is here. You should consider having a professional Facebook presence that you can connect, by way of this mobile app, with your university faculty or other user base population of busy researchers and scholars.

Apps like this to look out for in the future: Future iterations of the mobile Facebook app will probably feature data-intensive uses such as video chatting and perhaps media, too. One thing we haven't seen from Facebook mobile apps is product advertising; it seems that Facebook is pushing to innovate in this area, so look for advertisements, probably based on location and your interests, to start popping up in this application sometime soon.

Consulted: http://itunes.apple.com/us/app/facebook/id284882215?mt=8

FOURSQUARE

Screenshot:

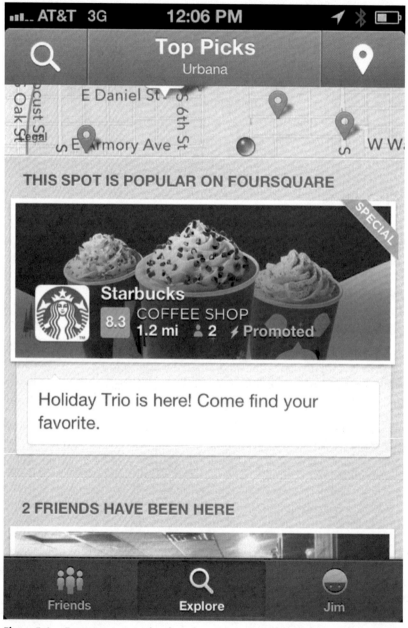

Figure 5.4.   Foursquare. Location-based suggestions and notifications are a cornerstone to the Foursquare platform.

What it does: Foursquare is a popular social tool that allows you to share your "check-ins" at locations like stores and businesses. Some businesses offer special deals ($5 off for spending more than $20, for example) for checking in at their location, which is a way of promoting their services. The mobile app has three tabs for engagement—a "friends" tab, an "explore" tab, and "me." Your profile is the "me" tab. You can sign in to Foursquare with your Facebook account, so you don't need to create an additional profile. From here you can also add Foursquare friends so that you can see where your associates are checking in and what they recommend around you. The "explore" tab will use your current location to suggest businesses around you for food or shopping, or other organizations, like libraries.

Use case: Libraries may want to create their own Foursquare deals and check their presence here to see what people are saying about their check-ins, since each check-in comes with an associated user review. Librarians in the associated institution may want to respond to or improve service requests from the comments about their institution on Foursquare.

Additional use case: Your library may have a mayor on Foursquare. Is that mayor associated with the library? If she isn't then your library has an opportunity to become the mayor of your library on this space. Post photos of your organization, list your website here, and also link to your other social networks, like your Twitter account. More about the merchant-facing toolkit is available from Foursquare's merchant page, which has resources for managing and engaging your library patron base.

What you should know/more information about how it works: This is a location-sharing app. If you aren't comfortable with sharing your location or interested in learning about where people have checked in, this probably isn't the app for you. Like many of the social apps reviewed here, this app offers integration with your Facebook account so that you can find and share your check-ins with friends as well as with businesses. In libraries this app provides another backchannel to engage library patrons using their mobile technologies. Your management of this engagement can come from mobile technology, too, but you should also make use of the merchant management tools available.

Apps like this to look out for in the future: The future of social platforms seems to rest in their ability to thrive in the mobile domain. One of the reasons that mobile is so interesting right now is that it isn't cluttered with advertisements. Startups that can figure out how to monetize a revenue stream from location-based check-ins are sure to make this an interesting area for innovation. Watch for more deals, and mobile payments, as well as more engagement with users based on location in the community.

Consulted: foursquare.com; https://foursquare.com/business/merchants

GOOGLE PLUS

Screenshot:

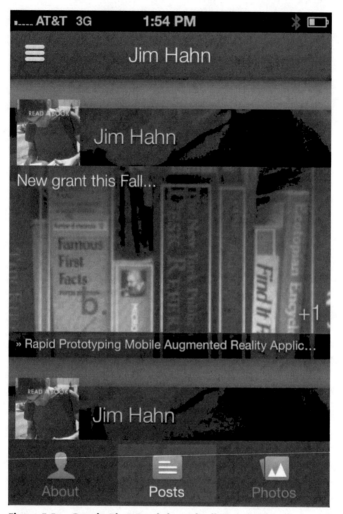

Figure 5.5.   Google Plus. Read through all Google Plus posts and information from the convenience of a mobile phone.

What it does: The Google Plus mobile app connects you to the content of your library's Google Plus feed. You can get mobile access to topics relevant to your account. The Google Plus social networking platform is similar to that of Facebook, although one area of innovation that Google Plus has charted here includes the "circles" feature. Using circles inside of a social networking tool like this allows you to share information only with those you want—you can create circles for acquaintances, friends, and family, and then any additional kinds of circles you want to add, as well. Of course there is photo sharing and sharing of links from across the web. On various blog pages, news pages, and other web content, there is the sharing service to "publicly +1 this on Google plus." This is the app that allows you to see what has been publicly +1'd, and also comment on and follow popular trending +1s from across the web. The "hangout" feature allows you to video chat with your connections from the mobile app as well.

Use case: This could be useful in larger library systems, and in systems where librarians are distant from one another. Should you find a need to video chat with a small team, using something like the hangouts feature will allow you to connect and chat through the front-facing camera on your phone. This would be useful for those librarians who are not near desktop systems or are not near an available wireless connection. The Google hangouts video chat could support quick meetings when face-to-face communication is essential.

Additional use case: There is included in this app the functionality to automatically upload any camera images you take directly to your Google Plus account. This may potentially be of use for activities happening in the library: special events like readings and activities would be captured and instantly made available from the library's Google Plus feed. Any of the library followers of the Google Plus page would be able to view the incoming photo feed in real time, as the pictures are taken. This would lend itself well to special events programming and onsite activities.

What you should know/more information about how it works: Be aware that video chatting works on mobile devices where you have a forward-facing camera. Also, the auto-upload feature of the images you take with the camera does not happen by default; this is something you will have to configure. Other than these important features of the mobile version, you can become more familiar with functionality of the desktop version of Google Plus; once you do this, most of the mobile functionality will make more sense, and you'll have a more intuitive feel for the app.

Apps like this to look out for in the future: Google is looking to add applications inside of Google Plus. These will likely resemble applications inside of Facebook, so in the future library development may encompass application-tweaking for services inside of Google Plus. Having a familiarity with the possibilities included in the mobile app version will get your library ready to innovate in any third-party apps that become a part of the Google Plus experience.

Consulted: http://itunes.apple.com/us/app/google+/id447119634?mt=8

LINKEDIN

Screenshot:

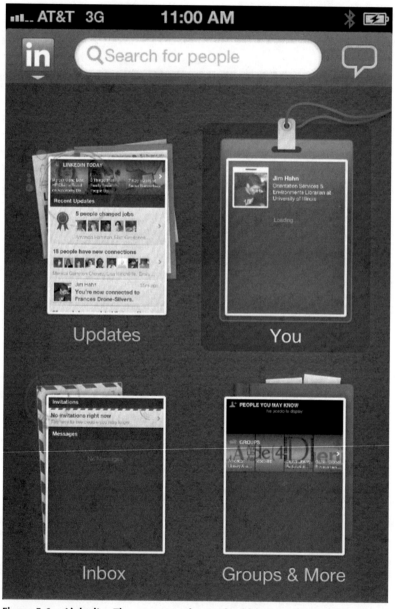

Figure 5.6. LinkedIn. The easy-to-understand grid layout and functionality of LinkedIn mobile makes it one of the top professional apps available.

What it does: This mobile app is the gateway into professional networking with the popular social networking site for LinkedIn. Supporting searching for users, searching stories, and messaging LinkedIn users, the mobile version of LinkedIn supports the desktop functionality as well.

Use case: Librarians are seeing more and more job-seekers at their reference desk. Public reference librarians will want to recommend this app, along with the Monster.com page, in order to recommend apps that aid in the job search.

Additional use case: The discussion boards are great places to network. By asking for comments and answering questions to professional organizations, you can help get your name into the public sphere and potential hiring managers or committees may seek out your application and perhaps even remember you—assuming your comments are helpful, well-considered, and correct to the situation. You don't want to make a name for yourself here in any other than a positive light, because the record of your comments will be preserved and likely surface in a Google search of your name.

What you should know/more information about how it works: If you haven't used the desktop version of this page before, consider this a standard introduction—the app works based on profiles job-seekers and professionals create. LinkedIn then enables you to connect with current and past coworkers as well as past supervisors. From here those supervisors can recommend you and say a few words about your past work.

Apps like this to look out for in the future: Probably no other company will be able to capture exactly the LinkedIn brand. Librarians who work with teen librarians will want to help new users to the social network sphere create an online professional presence that will be useful for securing jobs and internships during and after college—the mobile gateway into this network can positively impact future professional trajectory.

Consulted: linkedin.com

PATH

Screenshot:

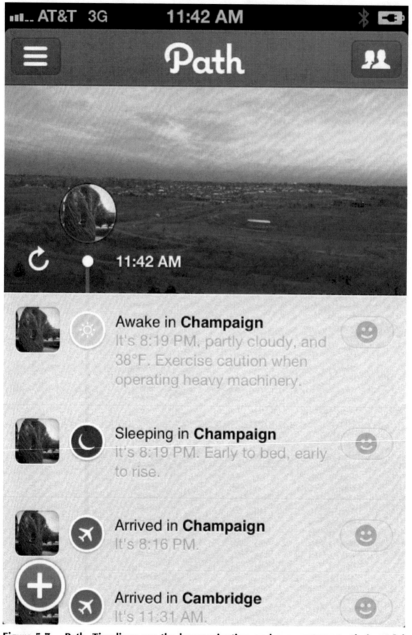

Figure 5.7. Path. Timelines are the key navigation and cornerstone to their social platform.

What it does: Path is a social networking tool to share information with your family and close friends. You can use your Facebook login as a login to the mobile app as well. What you do here is share everything about your day: when you wake up, what thoughts you have, and so on. It all gets collected on a mini-timeline view of your day—a "path" that makes up this mobile platform.

Use case: This is a more personal social app since it includes tools for documenting what would otherwise be called the mundane aspects of life—waking up and going for a run, for example. But could it be used for sharing anything useful among friends like library events, library books being read, or simply entering the library? Path also includes in a recent update a movie-sharing system whereby you can share with your group what movies you are watching and what you've thought of them. It could do those things, yes, one could share that on Path, but it wouldn't necessarily be a library service—it would be internal to a friend's list, a small and personal friends and family listing.

What you should know/more information about how it works: If you are familiar with the timeline functionality of Facebook, then the display of Path will make sense here. The key ingredient to the success of this app, or its uptake with the early adopter set, is definitely the exceedingly well done ease of use for being able to comment and enter in information. The icons are intuitive and offer simple input. Additional integration with Facebook updates and the pulling in of data from Facebook to help seed the Path profile make for a start-up account that takes little time—content is prepopulated from your past Facebook feed history. There is also easy integration with other components of the phone—you can, for example, make use of your mobile device's camera to update your cover photo, which is simple to do and can represent any current activity.

Apps like this to look out for in the future: Why are mobile social networks important? Is this a trend to look out for? By mobile social networking I mean applications that are only accessible from mobile apps, that do not have desktop versions, so they have to be utilized from the mobile device. And this is where the very personal nature of the app performance comes in—you have the phone on you, and you are sharing the day-to-day activities of your life. Perhaps in the future, there will be iterations whereby the app is recording this data passively, without you entering it in—you merely enable the types of sharing you want to do and then the app will passively, in the background of your life, collect and share this information with your small group of friends and family. Perhaps it means never oversleeping, never getting lost, and never being without company. But is this desirable—even if it is not yet 100 percent feasible.

Consulted: http://itunes.apple.com/us/app/path/id403639508?mt=8

PINTEREST

Screenshot:

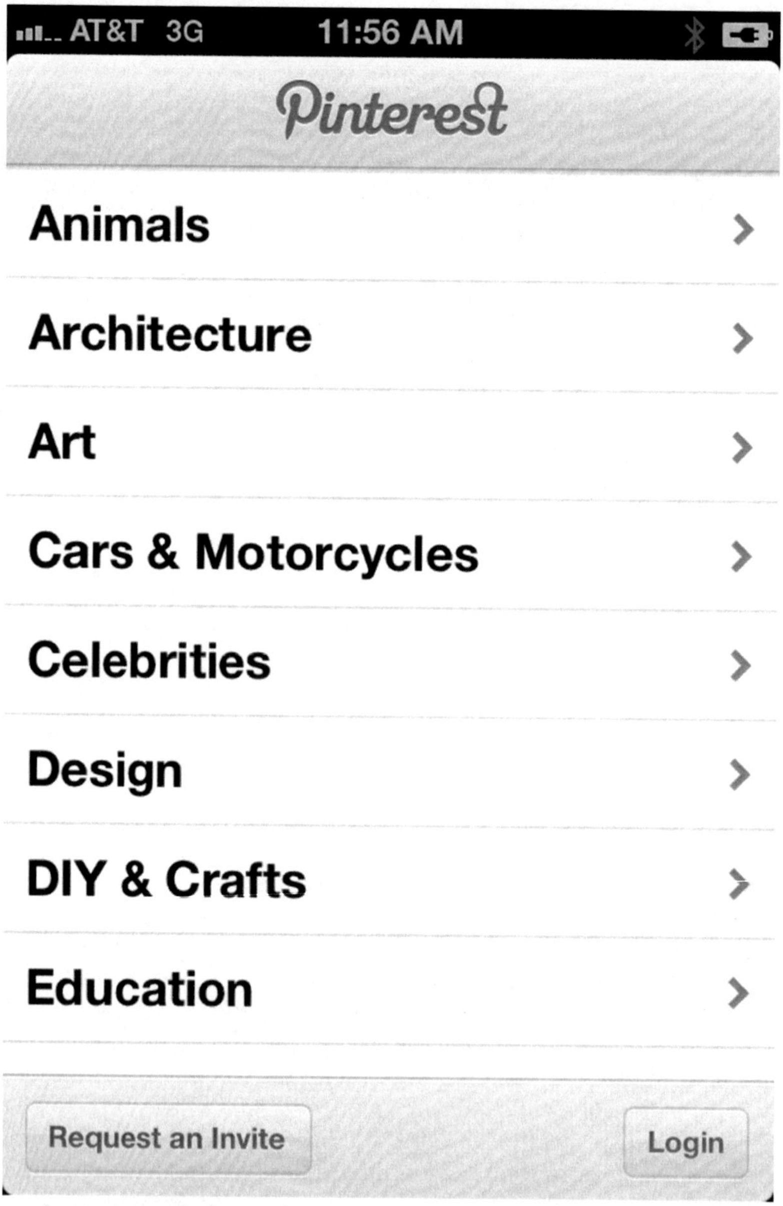

Figure 5.8. Pinterest. Sorting categories of interest by the commonly used list view makes Pinterest mobile easy to search.

What it does: Pinterest is a kind of electronic pin board where you pin images and make annotations of these images of interest. You create your own boards and add pins to those. You can follow others and others can follow your pinboards as well. The mobile app of Pinterest allows you to pin camera images directly to your Pinterest account. The app features a kind of login-integration with your Facebook account or your Twitter account such that you can link these accounts to the Pinterest app and then somewhat conveniently use one of those social platforms as your Pinterest login.

Use case: Collections are the domain of librarians. These Pinterest collections can serve multiple purposes. The first I'm going to address is public facilities–type displays that Pinterest could connect your user base to. This section is a little about why to use Pinterest, and then why to use the mobile app of Pinterest. Firstly, anyone who makes a display in a library will most likely want to share more widely the display. Maybe you take a few images and upload to a library blog for such things. One thing that Pinterest could do for your library is broaden the exposure of your library Pinterest feed—from this feed your followers could stay up-to-date on the displays, marvel at the physical beauty of it all, and pin it to their pinboards. Further, with the Pinterest mobile app, you could take images of the display being constructed and then post those in real time to a Pinterest board for your library followers.

What you should know/more information about how it works: The mobile version of Pinterest will not be able to completely replicate what you see in the standard desktop version, which is to say, large images and tiled display of many of the images in one easy-to-see presentation. This will of course be lacking on the mobile view, but the mobile view can support some interesting location-type information.

Apps like this to look out for in the future: Image-sharing apps like Pinterest and Instagram seem to have the ability to interconnect with many other types of social networking sites. For example, the ability to pin things from a Facebook app, and for Instagram integration to exist so tightly with Facebook, are signs that apps such as photo sharing and image commenting will be successful if they can support the third party APIs of the bigger social networking platforms. Look for apps like this in the future to be highly interconnected in the social networking ecosystem.

Consulted: http://itunes.apple.com/us/app/pinterest/id429047995?mt=8

SCVNGR

Screenshot:

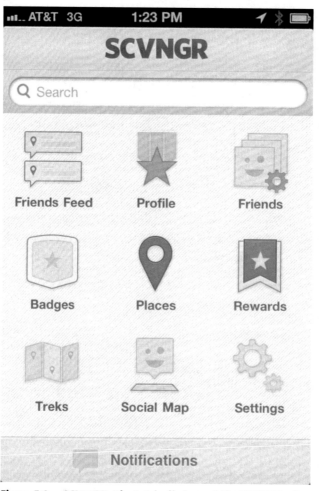

Figure 5.9. SCVNGR. The total offerings of the SCVNGR platform are in a simply thought out icon grid layout.

What it does: This is a mobile social gaming app. It helps users of the app explore their surrounding environment through games at locations, known as challenges in the SCVNGR setting. The idea behind SCVNGR is that it connects the mobile Internet connectivity with a location, hence producing a location-based mobile game. The main app screen is organized by the following functionality: the center function is the places function that identifies areas near you, other functions include a friend feed, profile, friends, badges, rewards, treks, a social map, and app settings.

Use case: A library services use case that requires a little imagination is to build inside of the SCVNGR platform. You don't have to be a coder to do this, you just need to think of interesting activities to do in and around your library community. Develop a trekking experience in your local library setting or community. As an example of a librarian creating a trekking opportunity, one could create multiple sites within the community to help new users learn something about the history of the area, and also some of the interesting and fun things to do within the community. Also, before you advertise the availability of a library-designed trek through the area, it makes sense to have some of your staff actually try this out and see if the trek makes sense or needs additional tweaks.

Additional use case: Award your library users by developing challenges in the library that are fun and engaging to users. Creative in-library users go beyond the typical finding a book in the book stacks; instead have your users do unique and interesting things in a library setting. This usually involves doing something quick and fun and also taking a picture of the result. Like stack all the red books you can find into a one-foot pile and then snap a picture.

What you should know/more information about how it works: SCVNGR is a platform you can build from. There are many games and challenges to complete based on your geographic location. You can, as an individual or as a library organization, contribute your own challenges to the app as well. SCVNGR asks to use your location. As a means to explore your surrounding environment, whether in the library or in the community, it makes sense that you would share your device location with the app, since without sharing, the app cannot locate you in the area and point out challenges, points of interest, or other features.

Apps like this to look out for in the future: Gaming apps for exploration are something to watch for, especially as location services become more commonplace. Consider also the affordances for gamification, which have gotten more exposure in library settings recently. To apply gamification techniques to library experiences and services is to create more compelling and essentially sought-after interfaces and services, where users are compelled to make use of resources because of reward structures that are built-in to interfaces and library experiences. Partly librarians will be able to design these, but only to the extent the platforms such as SCVNGR allow for it. Be on the lookout in the future for library service applications to platforms that provide gamification possibilities.

Consulted: http://scvngr.com; http://itunes.apple.com/us/app/scvngr/id323248984?mt=8; http://support.scvngr.com/entries/20299541-scvngr-style-guide

SKYPE IOS

Screenshot:

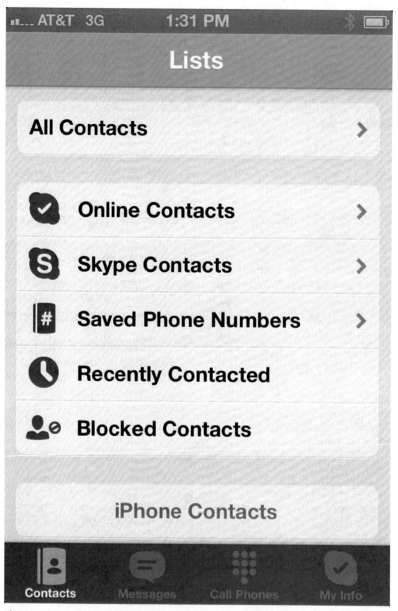

Figure 5.10.   Skype iOS. The lists feature provides easy and simple access to both Skype and iPhone contacts and supports calling to both.

What it does: Skype is the popular Internet phone/video calling service. It is popularly used to make cheap calls internationally, wherever Internet access is available. The video chat functionality is maintained in the mobile application. Some text-based use to cell phone and calling a land-line do require adding Skype credit to your account, so this isn't a completely free service. However, calling Skype accounts to Skype accounts is free.

Use case: Users making calls within Skype to other Skype accounts are going to be getting the best deal here. Within libraries there is an application in being able to connect to a librarian from the patron location, so patrons could connect directly with librarians over video chat from any location. Just set up some sort of mobile device outpost area where patrons are likely to need assistance—like confusing areas in the stacks or non-intuitive areas of the building. Let your patrons know they can connect with immediate help through video chat.

Additional use case: Video chat is a service that isn't currently utilized on a large scale by reference librarians. The opportunity exists, though, to truly meet users' information needs wherever the users may be, and on the personal device of their choosing—but we have to be on the other end, available and ready for video reference. It may be that some of the drawbacks of virtual reference may be mitigated when you are able to get visual cues from users. In essence it may prove to be a more useful distance learning tool than simple text-based chat. This is one of the possibilities with video chat reference.

What you should know/more information about how it works: Some IT departments haven't been happy with Skype running on desktop systems, as earlier iterations of the Skype app made it so that unused bandwidth was helping the network of Skype users connect. On the one hand this was helping to support what was essentially a free service, but on the other hand, having your network powering the calls of users who are not your own can be a troubling reality.

Apps like this to look out for in the future: Video chat in the future will likely feature more elements of interactivity, sending more bits of data through networks as they become faster and pipes become more amenable to video over mobile data networks.

Consulted: http://itunes.apple.com/us/app/skype/id304878510?mt=8

TUMBLR

Screenshot:

Figure 5.11. Tumblr. One of the most visually compelling app home displays is a key component to posting and viewing on Tumblr mobile.

What it does: The Tumblr app is the mobile version of the popular visual blogging service. The mobile app allows you to post images and video from your phone. From the app you can also access messages and reply to messages through the Tumblr platform. Additionally, the Tumblr mobile is formatted to display the visual blog content in a mobile-friendly and accessible manner.

Use case: Perhaps your library has set up a Tumblr account that offers users a visual and creative outreach platform for connecting your virtual audience with events, installations, and activities taking place inside of the library. These quickly updating spaces can now get information to your patron base even faster with mobile uploading of images and videos.

Additional use case: Alternatively, your patron base may be interested in creating their personal super-fast and easy-to-use visual blog. With this app, updating Tumblr and keeping a user base in the know in an easy-to-update way makes the work of updating Tumblr quicker and in a sense realizes the Tumblr mission of short, quick, timely updates.

What you should know/more information about how it works: The app allows you to sign in, so you need to do that before you can access your blog content.

Apps like this to look out for in the future: Most popular blogging platforms seem to be putting out mobile interfaces and applications now. The ability to edit and create entries from your mobile device makes sense, as long as the user is able to move information that was born on the mobile device (like images) onto that platform.

Consulted: https://itunes.apple.com/us/app/tumblr/id305343404?mt=8

TWEETDECK

Screenshot:

Figure 5.12. Tweetdeck. The app uses a column menu to help users integrate feeds from multiple social networking platforms.

What it does: The Tweetdeck app is the mobile app of the popular platform for management of multiple Twitter streams. The visualization of multiple accounts and actions from one easy-to-use interface makes this an app to watch. Features include a trending hash tag listing. You can add "columns" which are really lists from here—these columns can be a Twitter or Facebook account.

Use case: Managing multiple social network accounts on the go can be made streamlined and efficient. Responding to those in your institution's social circles can also be made more manageable from here. The value-add is that you can do this away from your desktop, either on a reference desk iPad or another mobile device that you are using to track and manage your social media interactions.

What you should know/more information about how it works: What you do with this app is connect your other social networking profiles. When those get connected, all feeds from Twitter and Facebook will be integrated into one master feed.

Apps like this to look out for in the future: The app may be at end of life in terms of social networking tools. How many more feeds get developed and integrated into apps is yet to be determined but aggregating social network feeds seems to be an early web 2.0 innovation and its further development into the mobile field will be based largely on how location-based services can become more innovative and original.

Consulted: https://itunes.apple.com/us/app/tweetdeck/id429654148 ?mt=8

TWITTER

Screenshot:

Figure 5.13.   Twitter. The compact and functional profile view of a user's Twitter account.

What it does: Featuring four major modules, the Twitter app connects you to people you are following in your "home" module. In your "@ connect" module, you can view your interaction and from the "discover" part of the app you can search hash tags (the # symbol, for the uninitiated) and keywords. You can also view trending topics based on those who share your interests. Finally, from the Twitter mobile app you are able to view your very own Twitter profile page as well as write a new tweet. The value-add here for being mobile and accessing the Twitter app is the ability to post photos you take directly from your iPhone to your tweet. In addition you can connect the location of the tweet to the update that you are posting (you enable this option, by default it isn't turned on).

Use case: Public and academic libraries are usually pushing out updates to their followers from a Twitter account. For times when you would be doing activities in the library, such as special events programming, or even when you would be on location somewhere, the Twitter mobile app could be useful for sending updates about the facilities in the library, or the locations in the community in which your library is engaged. You can do this by snapping a photo with a staff iPad or tablet device and directly uploading from the Twitter app to your Twitter presence. If you were interested in showcasing the community connections with your library you could geo-reference posts from your location with your library Twitter account.

Additional use case: Another public-facing use of the Twitter mobile app for library services includes the uniqueness of being mobile with a library device (or a librarian's device). You can be anywhere on location in your community and geo-reference library resources that tie back in to your community.

What you should know/more information about how it works: Sharing your location, taking pictures from that shared location, and posting to your library Twitter account are the unique aspects of the mobile app by Twitter for which you'll want to investigate service delivery. This resource, it should be noted, will have lots of uses that are non-mobile. The Twitter service is one that is deceptively simple, all it seems on first pass is a status update feed. Yet, it is more than this. It is a backchannel into a conversation to which one usually would not have access. So you should be aware of Twitter as a conversation tool, and connection to your community, or to parts of your community that may otherwise not be engaged in libraries. You will want to attend to this area especially for reaching out to new or perhaps underserved areas of your population.

Apps like this to look out for in the future: Design elements are getting improved. Recent updates to Twitter's interface have made it easier to understand the more specialized aspects of Twitter such as the hash tag, or the conceptualizations surrounding following and followers, which haven't been truly understandable to those outside of the social networking sphere, i.e., your late-adopter crowd. Look for Twitter to develop easier-to-use tools and interfaces over time, and become more design-friendly, as is its current trajectory.

Consulted: https://itunes.apple.com/us/app/twitter/id333903271?mt=8

WORDPRESS

Screenshot:

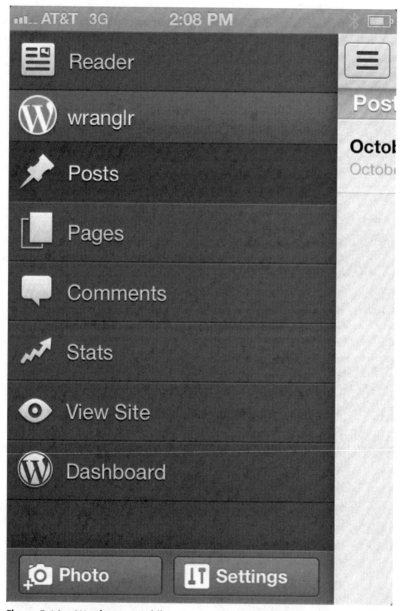

Figure 5.14.   Wordpress. Mobile access to your Wordpress dashboard offers comparable functionality to the standard desktop version.

What it does: This is the mobile interface for one of the most widely used and easy-to-use blogging platforms. Many smaller libraries and some bigger ones make use of the Wordpress platform as the library content management system for their website. The app is feature-rich, with many of the tools you would expect from the desktop environment. One nice aspect of the mobile interface is that you are able to take and add photos directly from your phone to your app. Other standard features you may expect from the interface include functionality to post, add pages, comment on pages, view your site statistics, and also access your global Wordpress dashboard.

Use case: In terms of apps that help for library services you could view a content tool like this in a few ways. One would be to view the library patron as a consumer of library content. Another would be to view the library patron as generating library content. In the patron-generated content paradigm, your library users would be able to upload pictures to your library blog around certain thematic areas, like book clubs, community exploration, or engagement. The choices of the individual library will vary but the common principle is one of letting users post their images to your Wordpress from their mobile devices and then also comment on those images. The library could offer an archive of an event in this way.

What you should know/more information about how it works: You need to have set up a Wordpress account previously in order to make use of the app. The Wordpress set-up is fairly easy and straightforward, and once that is done the user has access to a Wordpress dashboard, the place where you create and manage your blogs.

Apps like this to look out for in the future: Mobile content creation is seeing increased popularity—note as an example the availability of video creation and editing by way of a mobile device. Such functionality has been available since the iPod Touch 4th Generation, which allowed video to be shot and edited on what was traditionally a media-consuming device. Apps that help to manage content creation and sharing will be necessary into the future.

Consulted: https://itunes.apple.com/us/app/wordpress/id335703880?mt=8

Index

About the Author

Jim Hahn is the Orientation Services and Environments Librarian at the University of Illinois Urbana-Champaign. He has written more than twenty-five reviews and eight book chapters. His previous book is *iPhone Application Development: Strategies for Efficient Mobile Design and Delivery.*